Choosing Presence

Choosing Presence

· · · · · · ·

How to Access God's Peace and
Release Fear, Anxiety, and Stress

JIM HEANEY

TURNING
STONE
PRESS

I dedicate this book to my loving wife, Patricia, and our four wonderful children and their spouses. Also, to our ten grandchildren and, of course, to any other grandchildren we may be blessed with. As parents, we want to do the best for our children and give them as much as we can. I believe the greatest gift we can give them is pointing them to where they can access God's eternal peace, freedom, and power in the present moment. No gift we can give them in this world compares to that.

Contents

Acknowledgments

I will be forever grateful to Fr. Richard Rohr for being the one who pointed me toward the power and peace of the present moment through his many books, writings, talks, and our friendship over the last twenty years.

I would like to thank Emily Wichland, a truly gifted editor who edited the manuscript. Her suggestions, advice, and patience were all so important to writing and completing this book. Emily made me accountable for everything I said. I would never consider writing another book without Emily as the editor. One of the gifts of this book is that we have become friends.

I would also like to thank the people I gave the manuscript to for their opinions: Dr. Nicholas DiNubile, Stephen and Mary Jo Picha, Annette O'Connor, Pastor Jim Taylor, and Bill Reinl. They all gave me excellent feedback and suggestions.

I would like to thank Fr. Stan Bosch for his encouragement to write the book and also his contribution to the book, but mostly I am grateful for his friendship.

And finally, I would like to thank Patricia, for reading the manuscript over and over as I made changes and asked her opinion on so many things. Her thoughts, suggestions, and encouragement were invaluable.

Introduction:
What Is the Practice of Presence?

Imagine we had a group of ten people in a circle and each of us was going to write down what we think is the most challenging issue in our lives. In other words, we were going to talk about our inner fears, our inner pain. Each of us would have a different story to tell. But though there may be ten different stories in our circle, at the core each story is really about one central issue going on inside of us: inner negativity. Stress, anxiety, worry, lack of self-esteem—all of these are caused by things happening in each of our different life situations. And unfortunately, what too many of us fail to realize is that we ourselves are creating this inner negativity. It's not our individual circumstances or stories, but how we react to them in our unconscious mind that creates pain.

The practice of presence allows us to see clearly what the real problem is. It is personal, and it is simple to do because the power of the practice of presence isn't what we do but what is being done to us when we stop the inner negative dialogue and experience our vibrant inner life, which is accessible to each of us, always. That is God's promise to each of us: "Be still, and know that I am God" (Psalm 46:10 RSVCE).

The presence of God, the Holy Spirit, was and is the foundation of the Church. The apostles and the early Christians were energized and guided by God's Holy Spirit, the force within a person that is believed to give the body life, energy, and power. In John 4:24, Jesus tells us that "God is Spirit" (RSVCE), and in John 14:17, he says "The Spirit will show you what is true. . . . You know the Spirit, who is with you and will keep on living in you" (CEV). We seem to have lost our connection with this ultimate source of power. Our actions tell us we don't have confidence in the presence of God's spiritual energy, accessed through stillness, and that is only because we do not practice presence. How can we have confidence in something we have not experienced consistently?

Today a number of people practice Buddhist meditation. Others practice general mindfulness. Buddhism is connecting with the energy source, and mindfulness is relying on our awareness to fix ourselves. There are certainly benefits to both approaches. But what we are talking about in this book is much different. What we are talking about is the practice of presence, which is simply what God told us to do in order to have a personal intimate relationship with him. God tells us to bring in stillness. When we bring in stillness, we connect with our vibrant inner life, which is God's spiritual energy within us.

It is simple to do, and yet it has profound benefits to our daily lives. The practice of presence makes us aware of what is causing our inner fears, inner conflicts, and lack of self-esteem. Once we realize we have a choice, it is the beginning of the end of our self-created misery and inner chaos. That is the power of practicing presence with the intention of connecting with God's spiritual energy within us, which each of us has access to. No matter what spiritual practices we do—whether our daily prayers, reading scripture, or going to church services—the practice of presence deepens our spiritual lives. It does not take the place of anything or any practice but enhances every spiritual practice we do.

All of us are at our best when we don't have inner distractions but instead a sense of inner freedom. That is the core of practicing presence.

What This Book Is About

This book is primarily for Christians who want to improve the quality of their inner lives through spiritual practice. It shares with readers why the practice of presence is essential to connecting to and sustaining a vibrant inner life and—perhaps more importantly—it shows readers how.

The first two chapters provide background and context to help you understand why the practice of presence is so essential and powerful. In chapter 1 we explore the origins of our stress, anxiety, and worry, which affect our self-esteem in a very negative way. Once we clearly see the cause, we tend to ask ourselves, "Why am I allowing this to happen?" That awareness comes from the power of presence.

In chapter 2 we look at meeting God in the moment, which is what we're doing when we practice presence. How do we know God is really here, now? When we look back at our own spiritual experiences, no matter how fleeting they may be, we realize that God has been calling us many times to have a personal relationship with him. And it is becoming aware of those experiences through the practice of presence that gives us our inner confidence, our knowledge that we are not alone.

In chapter 3 we begin to transition from the why of practicing presence to the how. The practice of presence is all about stillness. God tells all of us directly that when we are still, we will know that he is God. We meet God in that moment. Stillness creates the space where God can teach us.

Presence is first and foremost a spiritual practice. Wishing for presence or talking about presence—or even reading about presence!—is not a substitute for *experiencing* presence. And it is not something we can do once and think we know what it is all about. To understand the power of presence, we have to practice it *every day*. The more we allow being present to God's spiritual energy within us, the more we'll gain confidence in its ability to transform our lives. This capacity is what I call *access*, and it's the focus of chapter 4. Access, which is the ability to approach God's Spirit, is everything. My experience after teaching the practice of presence over the last twenty years is that the biggest obstacle to our inner spiritual confidence is a perceived lack of access to our vibrant inner lives. This is a false perception. God has not made access difficult. We all have the ability to approach God's Holy Spirit, to feel its power. But it doesn't come to us through thinking, but through doing.

In chapter 5, we examine the discipline required to fully benefit from the practice of presence. Inner conditioning for the practice of presence, much like physical training, completely changes our inner confidence in our personal relationship with God. For many of us, for the first time in our lives, we know exactly why we are at peace and where that spiritual power and love come from. We also know why we are not at peace and, most important, how to stop the inner negativity and come back to our foundation of peace by doing exactly what God told us to do: "Be still, and know that I am God." There is no greater gift that God has given us.

God has made access to him simple, so why don't we all experience it all the time? In chapter 6 we discuss one of the biggest obstacles to God's presence—our own resistance. Resistance is at the heart of our anxieties and fears. We are in resistance so often that we don't even realize it's happening. Through the practice of presence that becomes very clear. Once we become aware of how often we allow resistance to interfere with our lives through its negative energy, we can start to dissolve it.

How many times have you said to yourself, "I have to stop thinking about this!" Unfortunately, when something is grinding away at us inside, we just can't avoid compulsively thinking about it over and over again. But this compulsion isn't something you have to accept as inevitable. In chapter 7 we summon the courage to stop negative thinking and gossip, pervasive sources of our suffering. Gossip, in particular, reflects our inner lives and the negativity and lack of self-esteem residing there. It separates us from who we truly are by inflicting pain on the people around us as well as ourselves. It sabotages our peace. When we inner-condition ourselves to the reality of this moment through the practice of presence, the compulsive, repetitive, involuntary thinking stops or slows down to a point where it can't penetrate our presence. Then we are free inside.

In chapter 8 we see that the goal of the practice of presence is to experience peace. Just about everyone has a goal in life they think will bring them happiness and peace of mind. We have so many people who are waiting for happiness and peace in the future. Unfortunately that future will never come. Peace is an inside job and can only be experienced in this moment—the only reality there is. But we have to be still inside because that is where we encounter God's presence—through his spiritual energy within us.

Sometimes we may feel uncomfortable asking questions about practicing presence. Some people may think, "I must be the only one who feels this way." That is not true. It is amazing to see that what we ourselves may think of as strange thoughts are so common in almost all of us. There is no question about practicing presence that is not important.

To conclude the book, I've put together a list of questions that have been asked by a diverse group of people— average working people, religious people, businesspeople, inmates in jail, homeless people, very well-educated people, and people who are not well educated. I've also included questions I have had myself. For each question I provide a direct answer to help you overcome a common obstacle or challenge to practicing presence. What has become so obvious to me is all the questions are so similar, no matter what the background of the person is. What this demonstrates to me is that at the core we are all connected. Hopefully this section will answer some questions you may have about practicing presence. One thing I can tell you from my own experience is that the practice of presence will teach you many things about yourself and who you really are—and how personally important you are to God.

The practice of presence has been primary in my life for the last fifteen years, and throughout the book I

Choosing Presence

share with you my insights and experiences. I draw on the Christian scriptures to show how the practice of presence is rooted in our faith. I also rely on the words of spiritual luminaries from many different Christian traditions to support my call to practice presence, including Thomas Merton, Eckhart Tolle, Richard Rohr, Thomas Keating, Anthony de Mello, Ronald Rolheiser, and Karl Rahner.

In addition I will share the experiences of ordinary people who have worked through the practice of presence—its joys, obstacles, power. While these stories are based on those I personally know and have encountered, I have written them as composites of real experiences to preserve and respect anonymity.

About the Exercises

At the end of every chapter is encouragement—a lesson, an intention, and a prompt to the guided breathing practice and three questions first introduced at the end of chapter 1 (see page 11)—to help you begin and sustain the practice of presence in your life. The purpose of these exercises is not for reflection but for creating stillness and accessing the present moment. When we start to have a relationship with the vibrant inner life always accessible to each of us, it is that experience that allows God to change us from the inside. Too often we try to *think* our way into a new way of living, but that rarely works. We have to *live* our way into a new way of *being*. It is the experience that changes us. It is not the thinking, but the doing.

The lesson at the end of each chapter provides a summary of the core message of that particular subject. The purpose is to remind us of the challenges in our spiritual lives—most often that we create for ourselves. Once we acknowledge these challenges and their causes, we can then apply the power of presence in order to help us overcome our inner fears and conflicts.

Setting a clear intention provides focus. The intention part of the exercise will ground us in union with God's spiritual energy within us. It is through the practice of presence and connecting with our vibrant inner life, when we are still inside, that God becomes the teacher. As it says in the letter of James, "You do not have, because you do not ask" (RSVCE).

The prompt to the guided breathing practice and three questions encourage you to try the practice of presence for yourself throughout the day. As we take three conscious breaths and experience how much less anxiety and stress we are creating because our inner awareness has changed, we develop confidence in the effectiveness and power of this method. Asking ourselves the three questions as part of our practice is an act of renewal. They let us know where we are spiritually and help us gauge how effectively we are accessing the presence of God's Spirit. Are we in the reality of this moment, experiencing the peace that is always present when we stop the inner noise, or are we allowing our unobserved mind to keep chattering away and getting lost in useless negative thinking? By asking ourselves these same questions again and again, we train ourselves how to find our way back to the present moment, back to peace.

By practicing the exercises consistently, in a short period of time you will be on your way to building confidence in the power of the practice of presence. As we slow down the inner dialogue, we realize we truly have a choice. We don't have to accept our self-created inner unease or chaos.

A Helpful Companion to Your Practice

To assist you in learning and developing your practice, I have created an app you can download for free to your smartphone (iPhone or Android) and use as a companion to this book. *Practicing Presence—A Christian Way* guides you step by step through the morning practice of presence, the breathing practice, and the three questions to help you gauge your progress. The app also sends you reminders to practice throughout the day, which makes the practice of presence even easier to do. That inner confidence we gain from a sustained practice can bring us through our fears, weaknesses, and doubts when our self-confidence and self-esteem are gone. It is true faith through the experience of God's spiritual energy within us, through the power and peace of the present moment.

If you find yourself resisting the app reminders, it is important to remember that is your ego trying to escape the present moment because it cannot live in the present moment where it can't control you through unconsciousness. In other words, our ego cannot withstand our presence, only our absence.

What This Book Is Not

This book has much to offer you in terms of helping you stop your inner negative dialogue and connect with your vibrant inner life, the way to peace that is God's spiritual energy within us. It is not intended to be an in-depth look at mindfulness or meditation in religious traditions or even a comprehensive examination of the theories of presence, meditation, and mindfulness in the Christian tradition. It is a highly personal call to a Christian-oriented spiritual practice that changes our perspective of life *now* because our inner well-being has changed. It brings us into the peace of the present moment. We know that we're not alone. There is an inner sense of connectedness. We go from believing to knowing. As God instructed, "Be still, and know that I am God" (Psalm 46:10 RSVCE).

Why I Wrote This Book

After fifteen years of not only practicing presence but making presence primary in my life, I felt compelled to write this book because while there are some people talking about presence, which is very good—whether it's in the Catholic Church, which is my tradition, or in another Christian denomination, the idea of presence is used quite a bit—I've noticed something, particularly in the jail ministry I've participated in for close to twenty years. I talk about presence and teach presence to the inmates. I stress practice, practice, practice. For many of them, their reaction is that the practice of presence is truly different from what they've heard in their churches. As one told me, "We hear about God and his presence, but no one ever said how we actually get in his presence—how we do it." I've also been a teaching elder for men's spirituality and male initiation into right relationship with God for over ten years, where I've come in contact with many good teachers, many spiritual men searching for an authentic relationship with God. And there we talk a lot about presence. But I also recognize very clearly that the real problem is that as much as presence is being discussed, it is not being practiced as it should, as God told us to practice it. We can't have random moments of stillness and expect God to change our lives. It has to be a daily relationship with God from when we wake up in the morning until we go to sleep at night—because it enhances every single aspect of our life. Jesus gave us an example of how to live our lives and experience a taste of the kingdom here on earth. We cannot access that without stillness, which comes from the practice of presence.

I have been on a spiritual journey for over thirty years, and I've had some very unique life experiences. At seventeen my life's ambition was to become a professional fighter, and then at twenty years old I was married and sent to Vietnam. And at approximately twenty-four years old, my wife, Patricia, and I started a family, and I also established my own business. I've been in business over thirty-five years. All these experiences have taught me that *love* is primary in our lives. And it has taught me some very hard lessons of how cold the world can really be, especially when you're struggling—whether its financially or emotionally. I have been a practicing Catholic all these years, and I've done many spiritual practices and all of them have been absolutely helpful in my life and in my relationship with God. But presence is different. You cannot imagine the effect it is going to have on you until you actually put in the time.

There are so many spiritual practices that we get relief from, and that's wonderful. But presence is beyond relief: It is a cure. As we practice presence consistently, it becomes easier and easier because every time we do, our inner well-being improves and every aspect of our life improves since we're no longer lost in thoughts and negative emotions and all that inner dialogue going on in our head, almost all of which is useless. In addition to the jail ministry and male initiation, my wife and I have done numerous ministries in our church. We've been involved in the Catholic Worker of Isaiah House feeding the homeless and also in Colette's Children's Home, which provides a residence for single women and their children. All these experiences have taught me that there are so many good, loving people in this world, in all our churches, but at the same time there is so much needless inner suffering going on.

I've been in business for over thirty-five years, and in my career I did not become successful by mistake. My success didn't come from being lucky enough to have my business take off; it was by grinding it out, step by step, over the many years without any resources to fall back on. These experiences have turned out to be a blessing for me. The journey has had a profound influence on how I live my life now.

I am very grateful to God for bringing me through my struggles over those years—not only the financial struggles, but also the doubts, the fears, and at times a lack of self-esteem from feeling alone and isolated. With basically nowhere to go for help when something went wrong, recognizing what worked was imperative. There was no room for poor decisions; mistakes were not an option. I have been successful for many years now, but the lessons I learned through those struggles are planted deep within me and prove invaluable. After all those years I have learned what really works and how to create a process to keep a company successful. The confidence and wisdom I have gained have been all God-given. Alone I am nothing. That is why the practice of presence isn't something I take lightly.

I knew through my own struggles that at times something was guiding me. It was only from practicing presence that I realized who it was and how close and accessible he was. I just couldn't figure out why he would love me. Through the practice of presence I experienced God's love for me and came to know that he loves me and forgives me even with all my flaws. Through this realization I also came to know that respecting every person who works for me or whom I do business with is not only a moral obligation, but a life necessity—we are all connected. If God loves me and forgives me with all my flaws, I am obligated to forgive all my brothers and sisters with all their flaws. Realizing this was a very powerful spiritual experience, and each of us has access to that reality through the practice of presence. It was easy for me to do once I realized that we are all connected. How can I hurt someone I am connected to spiritually? I don't believe that realization would have come to me without the practice of presence. Things simply do not work without respecting everyone around us, whether at work or in our personal lives.

Turning the management of my business over to my children was certainly a big move for me. It took a bit of adjustment to not be the boss and just oversee the business. I doubt the transition would have been as smooth if practicing presence wasn't primary in my life. The practice taught me and showed me something much better, not only for me and Patricia but also for our children. It taught me how to let go. It also helps that our children do an excellent job running the company with over two hundred employees and still growing. As I tell Patricia, there is only one thing on my bucket list and that is staying present. Then it doesn't matter where I am or what I'm doing.

The practice of presence is the answer for our inner suffering—certainly not because I say it is but because God says it is. If any of us could resolve our inner fears and conflicts by ourselves, we already would have done it. I've talked with hundreds of people over the last fifteen years about presence, and almost everyone I spoke to believes that God can change their life. But they really have not been taught about access. They think God is out there somewhere instead of right here now. God has told us how to access his spiritual energy through our vibrant inner life, and he has made it very easy and available to each of us equally: "Be still, and know that I am God."

Is This Book for You?

You may wonder if this book is meant for you. It is meant for any Christian believer or anyone who believes in God's presence in the world and in each other, whether Jewish, Hindu, Buddhist, or Sufi. It is not only for those who have participated in spiritual practices, but for everyone. What is important is our intention to connect with God's Holy Spirit, which is the force within each of us that gives the body life, energy, and power. It's not our spiritual knowledge, but our will to bring in stillness that allows everyone to have equal access. Jesus was asked by the Pharisees what the greatest commandment is. The answer he gave is "love the Lord your God with all your heart, and with all your soul, and with all your mind" (Matthew 22:37 RSVCE). That is the greatest. And the second greatest is to love your neighbor as you love yourself. And what he says next is so powerful: The whole of the law and the prophets depend on these two commandments. He is telling us that love is primary. It comes before everything. The practice of presence puts us in the exact space where God's love resides. It lives in this moment in stillness.

Following Brother Lawrence

Without Brother Lawrence, a seventeenth-century Car-
melite monk, we wouldn't even be thinking about the
practice of presence. His spiritual classic *The Practice of
the Presence of God* is a collection of letters expressing his
quest to develop a personal relationship with God. With
this book I'm certainly not trying to replace his work—
that's impossible. Rather, I'm trying to get more people to
do what he did—develop a constant awareness of God's
presence through his spiritual energy in our lives. And in
order to do that, we have to know how and why and what
the outcome should be.

So this book is a complement to Brother Lawrence,
making his wisdom of the practice of presence clearer to
the average person—outside of the monastic life—so we
can experience what he told us is most important: "All
we have to do is to recognize God as being intimately
present within us."

For the most part, Brother Lawrence developed his
practice within a monastic community, where he sought
to connect with God as much through his everyday
chores as in prayer. Most modern people aren't going to
practice presence as Brother Lawrence did—we're out in
the world, our spiritual lives constantly challenged by the
pressures and stresses of our ego-driven culture. As Carl
Jung said, 95 percent of the people are unconscious 95
percent of the time. We're mostly living through memory
or anticipation. Without a practice to slow down all that
compulsive thinking, to stay grounded in the present
moment, we will not be able to experience the power of
presence. In this book, I'm bringing in the practical side
of the practice of presence, explaining the work we have

to do to become present in the modern secular world and how to maintain our commitment to it.

That said, there are a lot of parallels between what Brother Lawrence teaches and what you'll find here. Brother Lawrence says, "When we turn our backs on [God], exposing our souls to the world, he will not easily answer our call." In this book we call that *unconsciousness*, when we're living a false reality completely out of God's presence.

As an antidote to unconsciousness, Brother Lawrence advises, "To be constantly aware of God's presence it is necessary to form the habit of continually talking with him throughout the day." In this book we do that by starting our day with a morning practice of presence where we connect with God's spiritual energy and, through that experience, we know exactly what we're looking for throughout the day. Then, by taking three conscious breaths with spiritual intention, we renew that awareness throughout the day. It's what Brother Lawrence calls "constantly guarding our souls": grounding us in the present moment, not allowing distractions to make us get lost in our thoughts. That is the practice of presence.

Brother Lawrence writes, "After doing it over a period of time it became so easy to do." Here we call that *inner conditioning*. By practicing presence throughout the day, within all of the activities of our lives—work, relationships, exercise, travel, etc.—it becomes easier and easier for us to do because we experience the power of God's healing energy for ourselves. We feel the difference.

In practicing presence, Brother Lawrence writes, God gave him nothing but wholehearted satisfaction. In this book, we call that *the peace of the present moment*, and it's what we're all looking for in our lives.

A Word about God

Throughout this book I refer to God, and in the intentions to the "Father," which reflects my Catholic tradition. However, feel free to substitute whatever names for God resonate with you and reflect your spiritual tradition. God is everything, so you can't be wrong! Perhaps you refer to God as "Mother," "the Source of Life," or your "Higher Power." The practice of presence is for everyone looking to put an end to their inner suffering, connect with their vibrant inner life, and deepen their spiritual lives.

The Practice—It's about Doing!

The practice of presence is about doing. There is a lot of talk today in all our churches about being present and how it enhances all aspects of our lives and our relationship with God, which is absolutely true. But there is not enough emphasis on *practicing* presence. Too often we tend to look for more information and answers instead of allowing the practice of being present to teach us through our own experience. It is the doing that changes everything. Without the personal experience of the inner freedom of presence and how connected we feel to our vibrant inner life, which is God's spiritual energy within us, we will not believe it can transform our lives.

As you read through this book, dog-ear the pages or write in the margins at the places that speak to you so that you can easily return to them later.

The main purpose of this book is to encourage you to try the practice of presence until it has time to take root. Once it has taken root, it is God's Spirit that leads us and teaches us. Then we will know what we are looking for and that we have an alternative, a choice: Are we going to choose our self-created inner fears and conflicts or the peace of the present moment? The practices are easy and accessible to all of us. The power of presence is not what we do but what is being done to us when we bring stillness into our lives.

Choosing Presence

An Explanation of Key Terms

Breath
As a biological function, it's the source of life. As a spiritual function, it's the source of spiritual life, our connection with God's energy. Breath is spirit. Assigning an intention to breath takes it from a biological experience to a spiritual one.

Ego
The part of our personality that feeds on the emotions and thoughts of the unconscious mind; that is, the thoughts, emotions, memories, desires, and motivations that lie outside of our awareness. In an unconscious state, our ego is insecure and fear-filled.

Inner Conditioning
When we practice presence consistently enough throughout the day—working up to three conscious breaths or more every hour—we become aware of how we feel inside. And then, when we sense ourselves slipping into unconsciousness, we know the way back to reality. Inner conditioning builds our spiritual foundation.

Intention
Focusing on the sacred purpose of the practice of presence means connecting with God's Spirit within us.

Presence
An inner joy and knowing that God's Spirit is here now. When we practice accessing that inner joy and knowing—that is, when we practice presence—we become still, and the negative dialogue that is the cause of our inner fears and conflicts stops taking us over through unhealthy emotions and reactions. In presence we can feel stability and security in this moment. No longer is our body in one place and our mind somewhere else, causing us inner chaos, because we know we are not alone.

Unconscious
Originating with our ego's negative energy, which is in opposition to what is real, the unconscious causes us to live through memory or anticipation and compulsively think or obsess about something that did happen or something that might happen. It is a false reality and at the heart of our anxieties and fears.

Vibrant Inner Life
The eternal location of God's Spirit within each of us; we need only access it to experience its power. The existence of our vibrant inner life is permanent—God's Spirit is always with us—but the prominence of our vibrant inner life in our everyday environment depends on the priority we assign to it and how often we access it and become aware of our connection with God's spiritual energy within us.

Morning Practice of Presence Session

We will start our day with the practice of presence and bring in stillness. This is our foundation, and we will keep coming back to it throughout the day. Begin each day with this exercise in a quiet and comfortable place, if possible, either sitting on the floor or in a chair, but always with your back straight. Aim to work up to fifteen or twenty minutes of practice. There are very specific reasons why we practice presence the way we do. For example, we put our hand over our heart to release a calming hormone called oxytocin.[1] Our experience is that it makes access to stillness easier and deeper. The way we take our breath is very important. And even more important is our intention. Our core intention is always to connect with our vibrant inner life.

1. Sit quietly and put your hand over your heart.

2. Praise God and ask him what you would like him to do for your inner self. For example, "Father, all goodness comes from you. Let your peace flow through me." This is important because it humbles us. We are aware that we cannot change ourselves without experiencing God's spiritual energy.

3. Take a deep, slow breath in, breathing deeply through your nose. Follow the breath as it fills your

lungs up with air. Expand your chest until you cannot take in any more air. (Use a sacred word such as *Yahweh* or *Jesus* to time the in-breath. Say "Yah-Weh" or "Je-Sus" slowly on the in-breath, which makes it easier to actually take that long slow breath in until you can't fit in any more air.)

4. Take a long slow breath out through your nose until all the air is expended. The out-breath should be longer than the in-breath. On the slow out-breath, you should soon start to feel stillness and get a taste of your vibrant inner life. It's when you start to become aware of it on some level.

5. Focus on the breath with each slow intake and each slow outtake. Focusing on the breath is essential in the practice of presence. When we are consciously focusing on our breath, we cannot think at the same time.

6. Continue breathing as you did in steps 3 and 4 above for up to twenty minutes.

When we are practicing presence and we are consciously present, there are no worries, no anxieties or stress, no lack of self-esteem, because none of that exists in the present moment. These only spring up in our unobserved mind, when we are unconsciously living through memory or anticipation.

Continue taking three or more conscious breaths throughout the day to access God's spiritual energy and renew yourself.

That is how the practice of presence teaches us—through the stillness we create and what we are experiencing inside. That vibrant inner life is our spirit, our inner intelligence, God's spiritual energy within us. When we start the day this way, it becomes our foundation. We know exactly what we're looking for then and throughout the day. That is the first part of inner conditioning, which is essential.

Important note: Continue taking three conscious breaths in a row, to access God's spiritual energy—use the *Practicing Presence—A Christian Way* app to help you remember. That is what renews us throughout the day.

❧ 1 ❧

The Unconscious Self

Understanding the Origins of Our Stress and Anxiety

> *I am just like you. My immediate response to most situations is with reactions of attachment, defensiveness, judgment, control, and analysis. . . . Let's admit that we all start there.*
>
> —Richard Rohr, *Radical Grace: Daily Meditations*

At forty-eight, Sam is a successful CPA who is happily married to Jill, and together they have two teenage girls, both in high school. He works for a large accounting firm that allows him and his family to live a comfortable lifestyle. Yet most mornings Sam wakes up at around five with his mind racing. He thinks about his job and the deadlines he has to meet—he feels overwhelmed with what he has to do and all his responsibilities. One of his daughters starts college next year—has he saved enough for her and her sister, who will start college in two years? There is work on the house that has to be done over the weekend, and Jill recently told him that she is unhappy about how their relationship has been going over the last year or so. She says that he always seems preoccupied.

Sam isn't even out of bed, and he's already stressed. Sam will be in a state of anxiety throughout the day, sometimes causing him to feel nervous and alone. Yet when his friends and coworkers ask him how he's doing, he usually says he is fine.

How many times have you had an experience similar to Sam's, where your inner conflicts and fears have sabotaged your day and you didn't really know how it happened? How many times have you lost patience or become angry with a loved one because of internal stress created by a work situation or relationship misunderstanding that happened weeks ago? How much resentment have you created by dwelling on problems over and over again and causing yourself misery?

You and Sam are not alone. About one in five Americans struggle with anxiety, and the reasons are wide-ranging. Part of it is financial: We've suffered the strains of a changing economy where, for many of us, our skills no longer match the available jobs. We haven't saved enough. And Social Security resources we were once assured of are dwindling. And part of it, among many other things, is social: The rise of social media feeds our compulsion to compare ourselves to everyone else, which puts our self-esteem in a perpetual state of compromise. It has also helped shift our culture to one that is less community-oriented and more isolated and individualist.[1]

I would argue that another significant reason for our anxiety is our increasing tendency to rely on our unconscious mind, which spins with compulsive thinking. More destructive than any of the negative influences in any one segment of our lives—professional, personal, social, or financial—the unconscious mind lives through memory or anticipation rather than what is happening *at this moment*. It makes us captives of the past and hostages of the future as it works to set up some other moment as more important than this one. The result is suffering of our own doing. We separate ourselves from our foundation—the experience of the peace and power of the present moment, the only access point to God's Spirit within us and our inner freedom.

What Is the Unconscious Mind?

Psychoanalyst Sigmund Freud believed that our behavior and personality derive from the interaction of conflicting psychological forces that operate at three different levels of awareness: the conscious, the preconscious or subconscious, and the unconscious.

- The conscious mind is what we are aware of in the present moment.

- The preconscious or subconscious mind is easy-access storage of memories. These memories are both practical and situational—it is how we remember how to get to work each day or our passcodes to our online accounts.

- The unconscious mind includes thoughts, emotions, memories, desires, and motivations that lie outside of our awareness yet continue to influence our behaviors. What resides here is often the source of our pain, anxiety, and conflict.[2]

The practice of presence has to do primarily with bringing us out of the unconscious mind to the conscious mind—from the wishful, negative, emotion-based, fantastical realm to the reality of what exists only within the present moment.

To live in the unconscious mind is to be physically here when our mind is somewhere else. It is a life driven by distractions, when we allow the situations to upset us emotionally both inside and out. Thomas Merton called this living superficially:

> When we live superficially . . . we are always outside ourselves, never quite "with" ourselves, always divided and pulled in many directions. . . . We find ourselves doing many things that we do not really want to do, saying things we do not really mean, needing things we do not really need, exhausting ourselves for what we secretly realize to be worthless and without meaning in our lives.[3]

When I was in the early years of building my business, my unconscious mind often ran the show. There were a lot of times where I was filled with deep anxiety and stress and I just didn't feel very good about myself. The pattern was if my business was doing well, then I felt good about myself; if I felt it wasn't doing well, my self-esteem was diminished. At times I had nagging inner unease, despite my outer success. I worked from 7:00 a.m. to 6:00 p.m. weekdays and often on Saturdays, and I felt guilty if I did anything personal during working hours. If there were special orders that had to be shipped, I worked even longer. Our family vacations were limited to Friday afternoon to Sunday evening. I refused to miss a day of work in those years. My whole identity was my business and its success. Too often I was on a roller coaster of negative emotions, all self-generated for no real reason. At the time I thought that was normal.

I found I frequently compared myself to others: Am I more successful than they are or are they more successful than I am? Am I smarter than they are or are they smarter than I am? Who's richer? Do I look better or do they? Often when I was with my family, my mind was in a completely different place. Even though I had a beautiful wife and family, I felt something was missing. I had a successful business but had a nagging suspicion I needed more. I was, as Merton describes it, living superficially, separated from those I love by the inner chaos of my unconscious mind. I was not *in* reality.

As I eventually learned through prayer and practicing presence, living in this moment quiets that chaos because it returns us to the present. The awareness that comes with practicing presence allows us to fully experience—body, mind, and spirit—this moment we are living right now and not what was or what could be. In this moment that we experience God's presence at some level within us, we are not alone.

Hitched to Our Ego

One of the obstacles to bringing us into the present moment is breaking our attachment to our ego, which lives in the unconscious mind and wants to hold us there. The ego is part of our personality that feeds on the emotions and thoughts of the unconscious mind. Eckhart Tolle describes the ego as "any image you have of yourself that gives you a sense of identity—and that identity derives from the things you tell yourself and the things other people have been saying about you that you've decided to accept as truth"—but none if this is necessarily true.[4] Tolle explains that the ego operates like a protective shell that separates us from our surroundings, setting up a constant comparison between ourselves and the other.

"When this happens," Tolle says, "the ego has you in its grip. You don't have thoughts; the thoughts have you—and if you want to be free, you have to understand that the voice in your head has created them and the irritation and upset you feel is the emotional response to that voice."[5]

Tony is another successful professional mired by the inner dialogue of his unconscious mind. At thirty-five, he is a rising star in an innovative tech firm, yet with all his success he is still constantly worried about his future. He wonders what he would do if something were to happen to the company, if they were bought out and he were fired. He worries about reaching his goals every month and what would happen if he didn't. He is constantly comparing himself to his coworkers, measuring his performance against theirs and wondering if they are doing a better job than he is. Despite giving it everything he's got, he only pushes himself harder.

Tony is liked by everyone in the company, and he and his new wife, Anne, have an active social life with many friends. They want to start a family someday, but Tony insists that he first reach a certain income level. His image and his financial status have become everything, which makes him routinely self-conscious and irritable. When Anne asks him why he seems so anxious and impatient, he acknowledges his behavior and says he's going to change. But deep inside he doesn't know where to start.

As humans we all want the same three things:

1. We want to feel good about ourselves; we want high self-esteem.

2. We want to have meaning in our lives.

3. We want to be loved.

The problem is that our ego sends us outside ourselves to find these things. Much like Tony, too many of us do not think we can be loved, respected, or accepted without some level of achievement. Our egos encourage us to measure our sense of self and our self-esteem by false images—our professional status or how much we earn or what kind of car we drive—and we take this to be our identity. But as Merton warns,

> None of us is what he thinks he is, or what other people think he is, still less what his passport says he is. . . . And it is fortunate for most of us that we are mistaken. We do not generally know what is good for us. That is because, in St. Bernard's language, our true personality has been concealed under the "disguise" of a false self, the ego, whom we tend to worship in place of God.[6]

We tend to apply the same false measurements we turn on ourselves to the people around us, creating negative feelings of judgment. By allowing our egos to keep us in our unconscious mind, we create a spiritual wasteland disconnected from who we really are.

The Role of Our Emotions

We all want to be happy, to be at peace, but the work-ings of our unconscious mind create an inner noise that makes peace impossible because it separates us from the now and the peace of the present moment. The inner dialogue of the ego stirs our negative emotions that then spin the gears of the compulsive thinking that cause us such anxiety. Of all our emotions, perhaps the most per-vasive is fear.

All fear is about losing something, real or imagined. We fear being wrong, hurt, diminished, or abandoned. When we let our feelings of fear take us over, we are once again stepping out of the present moment and giving over control to our insecure and fear-filled ego. As Richard Rohr explains,

> Fear unites the disparate parts of your own False Self. The ego moves forward by contraction, self-protection, and refusal, by saying no. Sad to say, contraction gives you focus, purpose, direction, superiority, and a strange kind of security. It takes your aimless anxiety, covers it up, and turns it into purposefulness and urgency, which shows itself in a kind of drivenness. But this drive is not peaceful or happy; it is filled with itself. It is filled with agenda and sees all of its problems as "out there," never "in here."[7]

At the core of all our fear is the fear of death. This was as true during Jesus's time as it is today. Jesus's followers were uncomfortable when Jesus spoke of his own impend-ing death, and they sometimes even tried to convince him that was not his fate, as when Peter "rebuked" him in Mark 8:32 (RSVCE). As Paul says in his letter to the

Hebrews, our fear of death can keep us enslaved our entire lives (Hebrews 2:15). I began to think about death more often when my wife and I started to have children. I came face-to-face with my own and my family's mortality. At the time, the thought of what would happen to my family after death caused me considerable inner anxiety. My fears subsided only with the experience, the awareness, of the eternal within as I was becoming consciously present. With that experience I became convinced of God's everlasting presence, peace, and love, of which there is no end. As we're told in John 17:3, "Now this is eternal life, that they should know you, the only true God, and the one whom you sent, Jesus Christ" (NABRE). Fear is always in the future; God's presence is always now.

Making the Shift

The solution to stopping our egos from controlling our lives only comes through a shift in awareness, from our unconscious mind to our conscious mind. Presence opens that door for us. When we practice with the right intention, we free ourselves from ego by reconnecting with the present moment. We stop looking for substitutes for our natural state of well-being within. We stop living through memory or anticipation—what was or what could be— and instead experience what is happening right now.

MAKING MEANING OF THE MESSAGE

As we practice presence in our daily lives, our awareness changes. We realize that not just some, but almost all of our inner fears and conflicts—our stress, anxiety, worry, and lack of self-esteem—arise when we are in an unconscious state, living through memory or anticipation, being led by our ego mind. It becomes very clear to us that when our thoughts become compulsive and repetitive, they become useless and anxiety-producing. If some of us doubt that that is the case, all we have to do is ask ourselves in those times of inner distress, "Am I present now?" The answer will always be no.

That is why the practice of presence is so essential. We cannot create inner chaos in the present moment. Fears do not exist in the present moment. Even if we are suffering, we don't feel alone and isolated because there is a sense of God's peace around the suffering. We are not alone.

Once we realize through the practice of presence that we have allowed that voice in our head, our negative ego, to control too much of our life, that is the beginning of the end of self-created suffering. Through the peace of the present moment we have a true alternative, a true perspective of reality now. We are grounded in the only reality there is: this moment—the only access point to God's Spirit within us and an intimate relationship with him.

SET THE INTENTION

Father, through your peace make me aware of the inner negative dialogue I create when I am unconscious and allowing my ego mind to lead me instead of choosing your peace, which is always here now.

PRACTICE PRESENCE

Bring in Stillness

Slowly, take a deep breath in through your nose, focusing on the breath as it goes all the way down to your abdomen and fills your lungs and you cannot take in any more air. This makes it easier to focus on your breath. Thinking and breathing at the same time will not do us any good.

Slowly let out your breath through your nose until all the air is completely released. The out-breath should be longer than the in-breath.

Repeat three times to access God's spiritual energy and renew yourself. If a thought should come into your mind, just watch it. Do not react to it.

Ask the Three Questions

As you slowly take a deep breath in, ask yourself: *Am I present now?*

Then slowly let the breath out until all the air is released.

As you slowly take in the next deep breath, ask yourself: *How do I feel inside?*

Then as you slowly exhale, focus on how you feel at this moment inside.

As you slowly take the last deep breath, ask yourself: *Do I have a sense of peace within at some level?*

As you let all the air out, focus on how you feel inside. Even if you don't have a sense of calm and peace at some level, just continue to breathe.

Every time we breathe it renews us throughout the day. Use the *Practicing Presence—A Christian Way* app to help you remember to take three conscious breaths or more every hour, to access God's spiritual energy.

Meeting God in the Moment

Getting Out of Our Heads and Into
Our Hearts to Connect with Spirit

The beginning of the path to finding God is awareness.
Not simply awareness of the ways that you can find God,
but an awareness that God desires to find you.
—James Martin, *The Jesuit Guide*
to (Almost) Everything

When I was twelve years old, I was an altar boy at St. Joseph's Church in Brooklyn. Many times I would serve at the 6:00 or 7:00 a.m. Mass before going to school. As altar boys, our job was to light the candles on the altar, fill the cruets with wine and water, and assist the priest throughout the Mass. I always enjoyed serving at this time of the morning because everything seemed especially quiet and peaceful in the church. (To this day I still enjoy early weekday Mass for the same reason.)

One morning in particular, I left church after Mass and started to walk home. I lived on Dean Street, which was only about ten minutes away. I was about halfway home when I started to experience this intense feeling of happiness inside. I became completely focused on how different I felt. I remember it was as though God were not only with me, but also inside of me. The sensation may have lasted only a minute or two, but it was so powerful that I said to myself, "Why can't I feel like this all the time? And why can't everyone feel like this?" I just knew that nothing was more important than what I innately knew at that moment.

Growing up in Brooklyn in my neighborhood, especially as a boy, no one talked about their relationship with God. It was sort of your own little secret. And as I got older, other things such as sports and girls took priority. But I can still remember the first time I experienced God's presence and how different that made me feel.

There is an innate human desire for a more personal relationship with God. But so many of us don't know how to get there and, perhaps more importantly, how to stay there. We look for God "out there" rather than inside ourselves. We wait for God to come to us rather than going to where we can meet him. We approach a relationship with God as a mental exercise—as a pursuit of knowledge—rather than an inner experience that frees us from identifying with the past and projecting our fears into the future. But when we get out of our heads and into our hearts, when we practice being present in the moment, we connect with Spirit. And in the stillness of God's presence we realize it's not what we do, but what's being done to us. We connect with a power we do not have access to when we are in our unconscious mind—the power of God's Spirit.

What Does It Mean to Have a Personal Relationship with God?

To have a personal relationship with God means different things to different people. To me, a personal relationship with God begins with knowing that God loves me unconditionally.

When I was twenty, I was sent to Vietnam. Within the first few months of my arrival there, two of my good friends from Brooklyn, Joey and John, were killed in action. To this day I cannot think of that tragedy of their young lives lost without tears coming to my eyes. The whole war was a tragedy. One night I remember saying to myself, "Here I am, twenty years old, I've moved from Brooklyn to California, I just got married, and now I am going to die in this [expletive] jungle and there is nothing I can do about it." I felt angry and hopeless.

Our spiritual teachers tell us that suffering and loss bring us closer to God. And they are right. In my despair I turned to a book that a friend gave me before I left for Vietnam. After all of these years, I can't remember which one it was—I have at least fifteen or twenty of his sitting on my bookshelf. But in it, Thomas Merton presents God in a personal way, a way I had never encountered before. He says that God created us uniquely and loves each of us uniquely. His words went straight from my head to my heart. Somehow I truly knew that God loved me on a personal level and that allowed me to experience God not only through the rites and rituals of religion but also in an intimate way. It explained how I felt that day when I was twelve, and I suddenly felt completely free inside. I somehow knew everything would be all right.

Catholic theologian Henri Nouwen describes a personal relationship with God as one we enter into without fear and ideally a two-way street:

> God does not say, "I love you, if . . ." There are no ifs in God's heart. God's love for us does not depend on what we do or say, on our looks or intelligence, on our success or popularity. God's love for us existed before we were born and will exist after we have died. God's love is from eternity to eternity and is not bound to any time-related events or circumstances. Does that mean that God does not care what we do or say? No, because God's love wouldn't be real if God didn't care. To love without condition does not mean to love without concern. God desires to enter into relationship with us and wants us to love God in return.[1]

A relationship with God levels the playing field. When a person realizes that they are supported by the power of love, as Merton says, they feel themselves "instantly becoming worthy of love. [They] will respond by drawing a mysterious spiritual value out of [their] own depths, a new identity called into being by the love that is addressed to [them]."[2] When we realize we are loved by God, we know we're not alone in our struggles. We have the courage to face our demons—and not only confront them, but allow God to shatter them.

God as Teacher

We all have struggles in our lives, and at times they cause us deep feelings of guilt and sometimes shame. We often suffer through them for long periods of time until we are emotionally exhausted, and only then do we get relief.

But even then the relief is temporary—the guilt or shame comes back as our inner traumas pile up inside. We revisit them over and over again, causing ourselves deep spiritual turmoil.

But as Jesus tells us in Matthew 11:28–30, God sent Jesus as the bearer of his teachings so that we don't have to deal with our suffering alone. "If you are tired from carrying heavy burdens," Jesus says, "come to me and I will give you rest. Take the yoke I give you. Put it on your shoulders and learn from me. I am gentle and humble, and you will find rest. This yoke is easy to bear, and this burden is light" (CEV).

The apostle Paul also reminds us of God's healing presence in his letter to the Romans (8:26–27 CEV): "The Spirit is here to help us. For example, when we don't know what to pray for, the Spirit prays for us in ways that cannot be put into words. All of our thoughts are known to God. He can understand what is in the mind of the Spirit, as the Spirit prays for God's people."

When we truly want to stop our inner fears and conflicts and change how we feel inside, we have to realize we cannot do it alone. The courage to face our inner conflicts lies in our vibrant inner life, in God's Spirit within us. That is our power source. When we allow God's Spirit of truth and love to guide us, our inner traumas start to dissolve along with our guilt and shame. We have a foundation of connectedness instead of feeling alone and isolated. As Merton describes it, we access "the Mysterious Power."

Jesus tells us in John 6:45 that we "shall all be taught by God" (RSVCE). God wants to teach us. He wants us to know our true selves, where we came from (Jeremiah 1:7–11), and the meaning of our lives. He wants us to know how important and personally connected we are to him. But God cannot do that if we have attached ourselves to the past. The past is not who we are now. God also cannot teach us if our minds and hearts are consumed with conflicts and fears of the future. The future is a fiction of the mind. Only the present moment is real, and only in this moment can we be truly aware of God's presence.

Jesus provides another reminder of the importance of being present in Luke 10, when he and his disciples take a break from their travels in a village and Martha welcomes them into her home. Martha's sister Mary drops everything and sits down in front of Jesus to learn from him. Mary is present to Jesus. But Martha is worried about all that has to be done, and she asks Jesus if he is bothered that Mary has abandoned her responsibilities. She asks Jesus to tell Mary to get back to work. But instead, Jesus says, "Martha, Martha! You are worried and upset about so many things, but only one thing is necessary" (Luke 10:41–42 CEV).

Meeting God in the moment is the only power that can unburden us of the mental, emotional, and reactive patterns that trap us in our suffering. It is only when we come into the present moment by slowing our inner negative dialogue that we can experience union with God's Spirit. By practicing presence, we replace our unconsciousness with peace, our insecurity with inner confidence, and our lack of self-esteem with stability.

The Role of Humility

It does not matter what we possess in this world, what our status is, or how important we may think we are. If we have inner fears or conflicts, we cannot have inner well-being or peace, and without it we are trapped in our suffering. God wants to resolve the fears and conflicts by inviting us to experience how personally connected we are to him. He tells us, "Be still, and know that I am God" (Psalm 46:10 RSVCE). He is describing to us that coming into the present moment is at the core of an intimate relationship with him. For many of us, it's difficult to admit we can't solve our own problems or achieve something on our own. And in that sense, God's presence is humbling. But as Benedictine oblate Christine Valters Paintner explains, even that humility teaches us:

> Humility is the fundamental recognition that we each draw our life and breath from the same source—the God who made us and calls us beloved. Humility prevents us from seeing ourselves as more deserving or graced than another person. It also compels us to recognize that we are no less deserving or graced than another. Humility draws us into mutual relation, through which we allow no abuse, no demeaning, no diminishment of others or of ourselves. Through humility we can let go of the quest for perfection.[3]

Humility challenges us to accept ourselves as we truly are; otherwise we will never be free. We tend to want to accentuate our good qualities and deny or hide what we perceive as our bad qualities because we mistake them for who we are. But as Thomas Merton writes, "Humility is the surest sign of strength."[4] When we practice being in the present moment, God helps us see that our negative actions are a result of our unconscious compulsive thinking. The stories our ego creates about us—and that we believe—have been driving our actions rather than what is truly in our hearts. When we are still inside, God's presence gives us the power to break through the illusions of our ego stories and encounter who we really are.

Where Do We Find God?

How do we know we'll find God in the present? Because God told us so. When Moses encountered God at the burning bush and asked what he should call God, God said his name was "I Am." He told Moses, "Say this to the people of Israel, 'I Am has sent me to you'" (Exodus 3:14 RSVCE). "I Am" is a clear articulation of the present.

And Moses himself is a good example of the power of presence. First, Moses had to be aware enough to notice the burning bush and that it wasn't being consumed by the fire. His presence brought him into a direct encounter with God. And second, in that encounter, God helped Moses overcome his insecurities and thus enabled him to rise to his true calling.

Helen Mallicoat reflected on meeting God in the now in a widely distributed poem:

> I was regretting the past
>
> And fearing the future.
>
> Suddenly God was speaking.
>
> "My name is 'I am.'" I waited.
>
> God continued,
>
> "When you live in the past,
>
> With its mistakes and regrets,
>
> It is hard. I am not there.

My name is not 'I was.'

When you live in the future,

With its problems and fears, it is hard.

I am not there.

My name is not 'I will be.'

When you live in this moment,

It is not hard. I am here.

My name is 'I am.'"[5]

We find God when we consciously come into the present moment, and it is in this place of stillness where we
grow in our relationship with God's Spirit. When we slow
down the inner dialogue and compulsive thinking going
on inside of us—the roots of our anxieties and fears—to
the point where they cannot penetrate our presence, it is
in those moments that we can be present to God's Spirit
and see what's real. But we have to get there, and we have
to know how to return there.

Only when we experience something different inside
do we act differently outside. This is the soul of all spirituality. Too often we try to think our way into a new way
of living, but we have to live our way into a new way of
thinking. It has to be an inner experience to sustain us
and change us. When we come into the present moment,
God's Holy Spirit invites us to experience his presence
and peace within us and around us in our daily lives. It
changes us from the inside out.

MAKING MEANING OF THE MESSAGE

As Christians, we all want and desire to meet God in this moment. But too often we're trying to figure out how to do that instead of actually doing what he told us. We have to be still first; only then do we start to experience a change inside. Then the power of God's Spirit awakens us to his presence. Over the years, many people have told me, "When I pray or when I'm in church at Mass, I don't feel anything inside." I tell them, "You may be praying and you may be in church physically, but your mind is somewhere else." As Christians, we believe that God reveals himself to us—which is absolutely true. But we forget that God is always in *this moment* revealing himself to us. Our problem is that we're rarely in this moment with him.

So how can we experience his presence within us and all around us? By becoming more present in our daily lives, especially when we pray or when we're at Mass, through the practice of presence. Before we are still, it's like looking out a foggy window and not being able to tell what we're looking at or what we're looking for. When we become still, everything starts to become clear.

SET THE INTENTION

Father, this moment is where your peace can be found always. All goodness comes from you.

PRACTICE PRESENCE

Bring in stillness and ask yourself the three questions to gauge your progress:

- Am I present now?

- How do I feel inside?

- Do I have a sense of peace within at some level?

See pages 10–11 for the details of this exercise or use the *Practicing Presence* app.

≈ 3 ≈

Stillness

Simply Doing What God Told Us to Do

Aren't you, like me, hoping that some person, thing, or event will come along to give you that final feeling of inner well-being you desire? . . . As long as you are waiting for that mysterious moment, you will go on running helter-skelter, always anxious and restless, always lustful and angry, never fully satisfied. . . . This is the way to spiritual exhaustion and burn-out. This is the way to spiritual death.
—Henri J. Nouwen

Imagine being in a wind tunnel filled with 48,000 small pieces of paper, whipping and whirling all around you. The slips of paper are moving so fast and erratically that's it difficult for you to grab them, let alone read what's on them and contemplate any meaning. And when you do manage to grab one, you see the words on the slip of paper are hurtful, demeaning, or simply gibberish. How long would you choose to stand there, being disturbed, frustrated, and exhausted by this seemingly meaningless chaos? How long would it be before it emotionally exhausted you?

For many of us, that kind of senseless activity is going on in our unconscious mind every day. Several years ago, the National Science Foundation reported that the average person has an estimated 12,000 to 60,000 thoughts per day—some experts estimate even more—and of those thoughts, 80 percent are negative.[1] If you use 60,000 as your base, that's 48,000 negative thoughts generating stress, anxiety, inner conflicts, and fears every day. It's hard to believe that these statistics are true, but unfortunately they are.

We may feel powerless over this senseless activity, but we're not. When we bring stillness into our lives, we stop creating the inner chaos. It's like flipping a switch and turning off the wind tunnel—all the meaningless pieces of paper settle to the ground to be swept away. We are suddenly aware that the artificial environment of craziness created by the wind is, in reality, a place of calm and peace.

We experience such stillness when we access the peace of the present moment. In order to experience stillness, we need to face our fears of the unknown and make ourselves available to God's Spirit. At any moment in the day, we have a choice: inner chaos or inner peace.

What Is Stillness?

Stillness is the gateway to Spirit, the force within a person that gives the body life, energy, and power. It is what we experience when we break the negative cycle of unconscious thought, emotion, and reaction that derives from living in the past or fearing the future and come into the peace of the present moment. Stillness is where everything begins. The Very Rev. John Breck describes stillness as sacred time when our mind is focused on only one thing—God:

> Only inner stillness enables us truly to listen to God, to hear His voice, and to commune with Him in the depths of our being. . . . Stillness . . . charts a way, a movement, a pilgrimage into the depths of the "secret heart." But once established in that sacred space, it reveals the presence of God and makes Him known in all His power, majesty, and love.[2]

Every time we bring stillness into this moment, it is a fresh start, a new beginning. We begin to experience an inner response of love and peace at some level, which intensifies over time. We connect with our vibrant inner life, which is unaffected by the pressures and influences of the outer world. There we connect with the only reality there is, in the present moment, and therefore the only access point to our true self.

Spiritual teacher Eckhart Tolle tells us, "You are never more essentially, more deeply, yourself than when you are still."[3] I know from my own experience that this is true. When I lose touch with stillness, I lose touch with my vibrant inner life. And when I lose touch with my vibrant inner life, that is when I allow myself to create anxiety and stress. Stillness brings me back into the present moment, where my negative compulsive thinking has no power over me. It is where I connect to my real power, my natural self-esteem and self-confidence.

Stillness and silence are similar, but they are not the same. Silence is the absence of sound. We practice silence when we remove ourselves from outside noise—we might turn off the television or step away from social media and find a place where we can be quiet and alone. Stillness is not so much about the senses—lack of noise—as it is about heightened awareness and intention. As Tolle writes in *Stillness Speaks*,

> When you recognize that there is a voice in your head that pretends to be you and never stops speaking, you are awakening out of your unconscious identification with the stream of thinking. When you notice that voice, you realize that who you are is not the voice— the thinker—but the one who is aware of it. Knowing yourself as the awareness behind the voice is freedom.[4]

In order to be present in the moment, to be present to God's Spirit within us, we must focus our attention on right now. We can't rehash in our minds a mistake we made last week or worry about what someone else thinks of us or be concerned that we won't get that promotion next month. Without distractions from the past or anticipations for the future, we are still and open to the power of Spirit. We are truly alive and fully ourselves. As wellness expert Peggy Sealfon writes, "When you enter a place of stillness, you awaken the divinity within you."[5]

When someone comes to me with a problem—or maybe many problems—and wants to know the source of this inner chaos, the first thing I say is "you have to bring in stillness, you have to become more present." When we seek to be at peace, we first have to face what is really causing the inner unease and the negative dialogue that stirs up negative emotions and reactions. It's always the same thing: We are thinking or obsessing about something that has already happened; we are thinking or obsessing about something that might happen; or we are resisting what is happening at this moment. To find stillness, to connect with the peace of the present moment, we have to ask ourselves in those unstable instances, "Am I actually present right now? Am I in this moment?" The answer will always be no.

At the same time, those moments when we feel energy flowing through our bodies, when we feel that everything is the way it should be, we have no resentments or worries, our self-esteem is high, and we are free and connected, in those moments we are always still. Authentic life has broken through and what is real is unmistakable because we are experiencing it now. That is the power we connect to in stillness.

What Stops Us from Stillness?

Stillness connects us to the love, energy, and power of God's Spirit within us. We feel at our very best when we are still. So what stops us from practicing it all the time? The fact is, some people fear being alone with God or don't believe it's possible.

If I go back twenty or so years before I started meditating as a daily practice—meditation is a form of practicing stillness—I can remember being very uneasy about meditation. I didn't feel as though I were worthy or holy, and I experienced guilt because of my own perceived unworthiness. I can remember the spiritual teacher Richard Rohr telling us the reason most people don't meditate is because we don't like being alone with someone we don't like.[6] There's a lot of truth to that. Even when I've asked people you would think had little faith in being one-on-one with God in meditation, they give very fearful responses. They somehow know that God is for real, and it just conjures up guilt inside of them. As theologian Ronald Rolheiser writes,

> We expect that God is disappointed with us and will greet us with a frown. The tragedy and sadness here is that we avoid God when we are most in need of love and acceptance. Because we think God is disappointed in us, especially at those times when we are disappointed in ourselves, we fail to meet the one person, the one love, and the one energy—God—that actually understands us, accepts us, delights in us, and is eager to smile at us.[7]

After people actually practice presence and experience stillness, their fear and their guilt start to dissolve. They come to realize, as I did, that while none of us is worthy or holy—our worthiness or holiness simply doesn't matter to God.

Many of us also find stillness difficult because it seems opposite to what is encouraged in our modern Western culture. We have an attitude that we must always be on the go, we must always be productive. We think that the busier we are, the more important we are. We think satisfying our need for status will make us feel better about ourselves. Instead, by chasing this external solution we delay living our real lives, the foundation of which is an intimate relationship with God. Spiritual writer Paula D'Arcy captures this modern go, go, go mentality in a tongue-in-cheek checklist she titled "Guaranteed Ways to Miss the Hidden God: How to Make Mistakes and Miss the Voice Within":

1. LIVE your life at high speed. No exceptions. Run hard.

2. STAY scattered and distracted. The more clutter and activity, the better.

3. TAKE everything personally. Never evaluate. Agree.

4. USE blame liberally. It's so invigorating. I wasn't responsible; *you* were. Everything's your fault.

5. DON'T laugh, especially at yourself.

6. STAY tied to your past. Elevate it to greatness. Live remembering and longing. Or missing. Why do it half-way? Go for it.

7. USE the word "because." "I can't change because . . . " Because is so little appreciated as a solvent for responsibility. Try using because. This *will* work.

8. NEVER question or think for yourself. Just keep moving and accepting. (Refer to #1 and #3.)

9. CONTINUE to think of God as invisible and distant. Surely not present in this room. At this moment. Not while I'm reading a book.

10. REINFORCE the belief that your life is going to happen soon. This is not it, not yet. But one day. Maybe when I'm finished reading.[8]

Our constant and often senseless perpetual motion is often our attempt to outrun our negative impressions, our compulsive thinking created by our unconscious mind. My friend Fr. Stan Bosch, ST, PsyD, LMFT, tells a fable of just what we miss when we choose to live unconsciously, outside of the present moment:

> One day a man found himself at the gates of paradise
> having just died. The angel of God came to greet him.
> She said, "Welcome, we have been waiting for you!
> Please come in and see what paradise is like so that
> you might make a final and appropriate decision." The
> man replied, "I don't want to make any more deci-
> sions. . . . I have decided all my life, and yes I want to
> enter!" The angel said, "Shut up and watch!" So for
> the first time in his life . . . the man shut his mouth and
> opened his eyes! He could not have imagined all that
> he saw. Off to one side of paradise he noticed beauti-
> ful and majestic snow-covered mountains with skiers
> rushing down the hills. To the other side of paradise
> he saw rushing streams of mountain water flowing into
> the lake in the village below, with fish jumping and
> dancing for joy. Then on the back side of paradise, his
> eyes were drawn to young children playing stickball
> and other games in the streets. He turned to the angel
> and said, "O angel of God, I could never have imag-
> ined paradise to be *sooo* beautiful; yes, I want to be
> here forever." The angel turned to him and responded,
> "This isn't paradise!" "If this isn't paradise, then where
> am I?" the man retorted. The angel responded, "This
> is the world you lived in but never saw."[9]

Stillness brings us into the present moment so that
we can see the paradise all around us. Yet we struggle to
bring stillness into our life because it means real change.
At some level, we all fear change, even when we know
our life will be enhanced. As Richard Rohr explains, it's

difficult to teach "Western wordy and over-thinking people how *not* to talk and *not* to think so much. . . . We really do like our thinking and our talking. It gives our mind and our mouth a job to do."[10] And we resist doing what is necessary to allow God to change us; it overwhelms us. But when we act on God's words—"Be still, and know that I am God" (Psalm 46:10 RSVCE)—we let go of the familiar way of living controlled by our ego and surrender to God's Spirit. This requires that we *trust in God.*

Putting our trust in something other than ourselves is also counter to Western ways of thinking, which creates a stumbling block to stillness. We pride ourselves on our independence, our "I can do it myself" mentality. We often view the inability to solve problems on our own as a sign of weakness. When we need to ask for help, we feel vulnerable and out of control. So we try to address our negative thinking with an interior search, but we won't find answers there. It's like having your car stolen and asking the guy who took it to find it. It is the unconscious mind that created the negative thinking in the first place. Only bringing in stillness—which leads us to a different consciousness—will stop it.

Jesus teaches us about the power of trust in the Gospel of Mark chapter 4. After teaching the people on the shore of the Sea of Galilee, Jesus calls his disciples into a boat in order to cross to the other side.

> So they left the crowd, and his disciples started across the lake with him in the boat. Some other boats followed along. Suddenly a windstorm struck the lake. Waves started splashing into the boat, and it was about to sink.

Jesus was in the back of the boat with his head on a pillow, and he was asleep. His disciples woke him and said, "Teacher, don't you care that we're about to drown?"

Jesus got up and ordered the wind and the waves to be quiet [Be still!]. The wind stopped, and everything was calm.

Jesus asked his disciples, "Why were you afraid? Don't you have any faith?" (Mark 4:36–40 CEV)

One way to look at this parable is our negative emotions are like the storm. They aren't real. The true underlying environment of our mind is one of calm and peace. We have to trust that God will settle our destructive compulsive negative thinking before it swallows us up, just as he quieted the storm. But we have to be in the present moment in order for this to happen.

Only through stillness do we stop the noise caused by our reactions to our negative emotions and start to let go of our attachments, as God's Spirit and peace overtake us and we see things clearly. Only when we see the workings of our unconscious mind as the cause of our inner pain will we come to recognize God's presence as the permanent cure.

Knowing Is Not Doing

Before I started to practice presence, I regularly asked myself two questions: Why can't I feel energized, alive, and at peace all the time? And where does all this inner negative dialogue come from that allows my mind to spin out of control? When I discovered through the peace of the present moment what was really going on inside, it stopped me in my tracks. Could it really be that easy?

The answer is yes, it really is that simple to understand, but you have to *do it* to *get it*. It's not about the answer; it's about the action.

Some of us already begin our day in stillness through meditation or prayer. But then we spend the rest of the day and evening without consciously bringing stillness into our life. That absence of stillness allows the stress and anxiety to build and our mind to start spinning, draining us of energy. But when we create space throughout the day for stillness, we return to the present moment and remind ourselves how alive we feel when we are in touch with our vibrant inner life. When we increase our awareness of our inner emotions throughout the day, we continuously break the negative cycle of unconscious thought, emotion, and reaction. We don't allow our state of emotional anxiety to build up and take over, essentially letting our unconscious mind— our ego—sabotage our day. Instead, we remain stable and secure in the present moment, the only reality that exists and ultimately our only access to true happiness and peace.

Creating stillness is as easy as taking three conscious breaths in a row to access God's spiritual energy and doing this throughout the day. After starting our day with the practice of presence, it is the most important spiritual practice we can do. It alerts us throughout the day when our mind is overstimulated and stops us from falling into unconsciousness. It frees us from getting lost in our thoughts. As we inner-condition ourselves, our body will not let us be out of the present moment for very long because it won't accept the inner chaos we create when we are unconscious. The inspiration to continue to create space for stillness throughout the day is the unmistakable difference we feel inside about ourselves and about every-thing in our life.

As Henri Nouwen says, "To gently push aside and silence the many voices that question my goodness and to trust that I will hear the voice of blessing—that demands real effort."[11]

If we say it's too hard or we don't have time, what we're really saying is that we don't have time to stop the inner chaos we're going to create in our unconscious mind living through memory or anticipation or resisting what's happening at this moment. We're saying we don't have time to allow God to stop our suffering. Creating still-ness demands real effort, but as we create space more and more throughout the day and inner-condition ourselves, it becomes easier and easier, until it becomes effortless.

We have to make time to connect with Spirit. With-out inner-conditioning ourselves through the simple practices, we won't get very far. Becoming still inside and slowing down or stopping all the inner negative dialogue gives us a choice. This practice gives us a true perspec-tive of reality now. We give ourselves a clear contrast of stillness versus unconsciousness. Then it's an easy choice.

MAKING MEANING OF THE MESSAGE

Stillness is the foundation of the practice of presence. God tells us in Psalm 46:10 to "be still, and know that I am God." When we read it, it should become clear to us that it is not a suggestion; it is a command. Therefore, stillness is our foundation. Without it we will not experi-ence God's Spirit within us. We will not know him in an intimate way. And that is the heart and soul of the practice of presence. The practice teaches us through stillness. It is only when we become still inside that we connect with our vibrant inner life, which is our inner intelligence, and it comes from God's Spirit within us. That is what we are looking for. We cannot experience the peace of the present moment without some level of stillness inside. That is what builds our inner confidence, our foundation. When we're dealing with any distress, no matter what it is, our first response should be to bring in stillness. By bringing in stillness we get a true perspective of our life now because the screen of our ego is not distorting reality. The practice of presence lets us know that we are not alone and isolated. And the only time we do feel alone and isolated is when we are unconscious, living through memory or anticipation in a compulsively negative thinking state.

SET THE INTENTION

Father, please help me to become still so that I may experience your spiritual energy within me.

PRACTICE PRESENCE

Bring in stillness and ask yourself the three questions to gauge your progress:

- Am I present now?

- How do I feel inside?

- Do I have a sense of peace within at some level?

See pages 10–11 for the details of this exercise or use the *Practicing Presence* app.

≈ 4 ≈

Accessing Presence

*Being in the Space Where We Know
That God Is Here Now*

The present contains all that there is. It is holy ground.
—Alfred North Whitehead

What have we learned so far?
We know that our inner conflicts and fears stem from our ego, our unconscious mind. The negative dialogue it generates is fixated on something that happened in the past or something we anticipate happening in the future. It keeps us from encountering God in the present moment because our minds and hearts are somewhere else. We are not in reality, and we're suffering.

We know we want to have a deep relationship with God because it is when we feel connected to him that we are truly ourselves. God's unconditional love releases us from our negative inner dialogue and allows us to see our struggles for what they really are—primarily created by us. In God's presence we are able to see what's real, and that frees us from our suffering.

Stillness is the gateway to God. We know that when we still our minds, we break the negative cycle of unconscious thought, emotion, and reaction that derives from living in the past or fearing the future, and we come into the present moment. God is in the present moment; therefore, stillness connects us to the love, energy, and power of God's Spirit within us.

But knowing all of this is not enough. My sharing this information with you is not enough. Presence is first and foremost a spiritual *practice*. It is not something we can wish for or just talk about and expect to reap its benefits. And it is not something we can do once and think we know what it is all about. For us to truly understand the power of being present, we have to get in the habit of doing it every day. And as with anything we work at, the more we practice being present, the more we'll gain confidence in its power to transform our lives.

Presence Is a Spiritual Practice

Spiritual practices are at the core of all the world's religions. Prayer, meditation, chant, yoga, and many other options—these are all ways our faith traditions train us to merge our bodies and minds in order to connect with our vibrant inner life. As Christian theologian Richard J. Foster writes in *Life with God*, "A spiritual [practice] is an intentionally directed action which places us in a position to receive from God the power to do what we cannot accomplish on our own."[1]

Some spiritual practices such as the sacrament of the Eucharist are complex and deeply rooted in theology. Other spiritual practices are relatively simple—the act of assigning intention to everyday activities as a way to improve our spiritual well-being, such as mindful gardening or walking.

Regardless of their intricacies, what all spiritual practices have in common is *action*. As wellness writer and holistic lifestyle consultant Maggie Lyon writes,

> The practice part means just that: you do it daily, over and over, not in a gross way, but rather in a this-is-what-makes-me-who-I-am way. Without the aim of ever stopping with it, you practice as contribution to your ever-unfolding life on this earth. It can feel beautiful and compelling, harrowing and agonizing, annoying, vexing, boring as hell or as ordinary and routine as brushing your teeth. Above all it is your rock, the ultimate placating pillar, steady and reliable as they come."[2]

In my experience, there isn't a spiritual practice simpler or more powerful than practicing presence. Presence is a spiritual practice that we can do every day, many times throughout the day, to ground ourselves in the moment. Anyone can do it because its foundation is the breath.

How does it work? We begin our day with the practice of presence by consciously breathing and bringing in stillness as a way of grounding ourselves in reality. Some may describe this as meditation or an extended practice of presence. As we do this, our compulsive thinking slows, our negative inner dialogue dissolves to the point where it cannot penetrate our peace, and our inner conflicts no longer have power over us. This is our foundation for how we want to feel throughout the day—in the present moment, in the presence of God's Spirit. We tap into our inner well-being and acknowledge, "This is me at peace." We begin each day knowing exactly what we're looking for inside.

Then throughout the day we return to the breath. By this I mean we take three or more deep, intentional breaths every hour—or more—throughout the day to keep us close to the present moment. The closer we are to the present moment, the less energy we give to our destructive inner negative dialogue. It doesn't have time to build up and create the suffering we experience when we're outside of the present moment.

As the Jesuit priest Anthony de Mello writes in *The Heart of the Enlightened*, "The present moment is never unbearable if you live in it fully. What is unbearable is to have your body here at 10 a.m. and your mind at 6 p.m."[3]

Once we become still inside, our job is to listen. This is an important distinction between practicing presence and practicing prayer. Presence and prayer are similar in that we do them with the intention of connecting with God's Spirit within us, which gives meaning to our lives. When we pray properly and when we become still inside, we experience our vibrant inner life. We know we are not alone. And both blend into each other because they are done with the right intention.

But prayer is an action of asking, of reaching out to God, whereas presence is an action of listening for what God has to teach us when all the inner noise stops distracting us. It is about receiving the courage to face our flaws and listening for God's forgiveness, which, in turn, enables us to forgive ourselves. In this way presence isn't a feel-good exercise—it goes beyond feeling good. As Saint Augustine of Hippo wrote, "The love that is poured into our hearts by the holy spirit is its very self the forgiveness of sins."[4] Not only do we experience peace, but we also know how to get back to peace when we fall out of it. This makes the spiritual practice of presence not just a relief, but a cure. We have the choice of constant renewal.

Does presence take the place of other spiritual practices such as prayer? No, but it deepens and enhances all our other practices, including prayer. Years ago, when I first started to practice presence, I realized one night that I was saying the Our Father with other thoughts coming through my mind at the same time. So after I finished, I said it again, but this time very slowly, focusing on every word. It was a completely different experience. All the words became alive. As James says, if we pray to God in two minds, we shouldn't expect anything from God (James 1:7–8). How can God give me an answer to what I am praying for if I'm not where he is—right here, now? Three or more deep, intentional breaths bring us into the present where we can experience God's Spirit and power within us.

Our ego might say that it is too easy, that practicing presence in this way doesn't have the power to change us. But God always makes access to him simple. Through that simplicity flows God's peace, wisdom, and love. It is God hiding in plain sight.

Breath as Healer

How can something as simple as breathing become such a powerful spiritual experience? The breath has a long history of being central to spirit and healing—in fact, it goes back to the beginning. In the Judeo-Christian tradition alone there are many scriptural references that present the breath as a gift from God. Breath is the life force in the book of Genesis—"a wind [breath] from God swept over the face of the waters" (1:2 NRSV); "and God breathed life into man" (2:7 CEV). In John 20:22, Jesus appears to his apostles after the resurrection and breathes on them, saying "Receive the Holy Spirit" (RSVCE).

Interestingly, the Greek for "Holy Spirit," *agia pneuma*, can also be translated as "Holy Breath." *Ruach*, in Hebrew, can be translated as meaning both "breath" and "spirit." As Fr. William Johnston writes in *Christian Zen*,

> In the Bible it is clear that breath is identified with the deepest thing in man; it is precisely when breath enters into matter that man becomes man. . . . For the Hebrews, they believed that their breath was the breath of God whose presence gave them life. For Christians, the breath, like the wind, symbolizes the Holy Spirit who fills all things with his love, giving wisdom and joy and peace. . . .[5]

Breath is Spirit! And I feel it when I surrender to its power and stop the inner chaos created in my unconscious mind so that I can rest in reality. There are times when I find myself feeling anxious or impatient about some issue I have to deal with. As I focus on my breath, it may take a few minutes to stop the inner dialogue, but eventually I come to an intense sense of calm and peace that completely takes me over. Whatever was triggering anxiety or impatience surrenders to the deep peace and love I am experiencing within. It's then that I know I'm in the presence of God's Spirit.

MAKING MEANING OF THE MESSAGE

Access is everything, and God tells us exactly how to access the present moment where he resides always. He tells us, "Be still, and know that I am God." When we read that or say it, it seems almost too good to be true. But when we practice presence through the breath and bring in stillness, our own experience teaches us it is exactly so. God has made access easy and available to each of us equally. What we have to do is stop allowing our insecure and unstable ego to lead us and take us out of reality. The access point is not our head, but our heart. And being in the present moment opens our heart because all the distractions have stopped. We are present to the only reality there is: this moment now.

SET THE INTENTION

Father, you have given me and all of us access to your presence. And that humbles me.

PRACTICE PRESENCE

Bring in stillness and ask yourself the three questions to gauge your progress:

- Am I present now?

- How do I feel inside?

- Do I have a sense of peace within at some level?

See pages 10–11 for the details of this exercise or use the *Practicing Presence* app.

⪦ 5 ⪧

Inner Conditioning

Building Our Foundation on Rock

*The present moment holds infinite riches beyond your
wildest dreams but you will only enjoy them to the extent
of your faith and love. The more a soul loves, the more it
longs, the more it hopes, the more it finds.*

—Jean-Pierre de Caussade, SJ

Human beings are creatures of habit. We work our
way into routines for everything from eating to
sleeping to getting to and from work. Sure, all of us have
some negative habits, but we also keep many good ones—
we may go to the gym every day or regularly say "thank
you," for example. Once a habit is ingrained, we rarely
put any thought into why we do it or its usefulness in our
lives. In mind and body, we just do it.

Through practicing presence, we are essentially training ourselves to recognize when we're at peace and when
we're not at peace. We're forming a habit of being aware
of how we feel inside. And when we detect that we are
not at peace—perhaps our minds are racing with negative

thinking, our self-esteem is low, or our muscles are tense with stress—we know how to find our way back to peace. We take several deep intentional breaths and restore ourselves to the present moment where our vibrant inner life connects us to reality *now*.

I call this interplay *contrast and choice*. The experience of presence provides us a contrast in order to clearly realize the difference between our inner well-being when we are present in this moment versus when we are living through memory or anticipation, being led unconsciously by our ego and emotions. Without experiencing the contrast—that unmistakable difference in our well-being—we may be able to identify that we're suffering, but we won't know the way out of it. When we practice presence, we know the path out of our suffering, and it is our choice whether to follow that path. Fear is always in the future; inner freedom and peace are always *now*.

Over fifteen years ago I had a conversation with Richard Rohr, and what he said had such a profound effect on me in pointing me in the right direction. Patricia and I had attended a talk Richard was giving on the topic of presence. Afterward we were talking about the presentation, and I said to him, "Richard, what exactly do you mean by presence?" He answered, "Jim, presence is everything." *Everything*, to me, was such a powerful word coming from Richard—everything is *everything*.

That experience with Richard was a turning point in how I practice presence. Prior to Richard saying that, I had been meditating for seven or eight years at that point and studying about presence and trying to practice presence. When Richard said that, I knew for the first time that I had to make presence primary in my life, which completely changed my experience of presence from all in my head and trying to figure it out to, over the next four or five months, experiencing my vibrant inner life on a deeper and deeper level. I finally knew exactly what I was looking for, and when I wasn't present, I knew how to get back to being present. And I just instinctively knew that I was not alone. It was and is the single most powerful thing in my life—as Richard said, it's everything; he was 100 percent correct. Every day it truly is a new beginning regardless of what problems or life situations I may have. It is the power we all have access to through God's grace.

Presence is everything simply because when we are not consciously present, we are not in reality, now. And when we're not in reality, now, that's when we unconsciously create our inner fears and conflicts.

For me, there is nothing more important than being aware of my inner life. I can choose either the peace of the present moment or the inner chaos of unconsciousness. By regularly practicing presence, I have conditioned my body to alert me when I am slipping out of reality. At that moment I can take a few deep, intentional breaths and stop the negative thoughts before they turn to emotions and subsequently into negative reactions. It is God's grace at work. It can be the same for anyone who consciously practices presence.

Whether it's a sports, music, art, or professional skill, it takes practice to get good at something. When we start experiencing the benefits of a practice, we gain confidence in it and our ability to benefit from it. Practicing presence is no different. If we want to know inner peace, we have to do the work necessary to bring in stillness that puts us in the space where we can experience God's Spirit. But we also have to be willing to embrace change in how we typically view and cope with our anxiety, fears, and stress. And as with anything, change doesn't always come easily.

My company manufactures medical equipment for injury rehabilitation and pain control. Years ago, Paula, a medical salesperson, approached me with a marketing plan she wanted to implement with our product. And after talking with her over a period of months and months—probably over a year—I finally said okay and agreed to sit down with her about it. She came in very excited, very knowledgeable, and the plan seemed like it could be effective. I already knew she was an excellent salesperson, so I told her we would implement the plan. She set up a series of appointments over a one-week period, and just before the plan was ready to roll out, she asked me who would be accompanying her to treat the patients. I said, "Actually, I'm going with you on all the sales presentations, and I'm going to teach you how to do the treatments."

Paula was visibly shocked. I explained to her that there was nothing to worry about, the training would not only teach her more about our product, but she would also become a more effective salesperson. But she was initially unable to change her way of thinking and how she had perceived going about these sales calls, and by the next day she was physically ill. She had to go to the doctor, and we put off the appointments for a week. But once we spent a week together, every day she became a little more confident, and by the end of the week she was a completely different person. Not only did she have confidence in her marketing and sales skills, but she also had experience and could trust in the actual application of what she was talking about.

As with Paula, we all tend to fall into a state of inner fear when faced with change. Even when we know we are going to continue to fail, we are often reluctant to change course. So the big question remains: Where do we get the courage to change? With God, as spiritual writer Debra Moffitt explains,

> Courage literally means to take something to heart. Strength is found in the depths of the heart. Sometimes we need to excavate and go deep to find it. The more deeply we feel that we are One with the Divine or Love or whatever you want to call it, the more we become fearless. . . . [Courage] is rooted in your deep connection to the Divine. By focusing on this connection, self-confidence and inner strength develop. Nothing can deter you from moving in the direction your heart carries you.[1]

In Pursuit of Peace

Lasting inner peace is a tall order. It's an immense, almost overwhelming goal. However, if you know how to identify when you're at peace and when you're not at peace and you know how to return to inner peace, you have achieved that end.

However, too often spiritual seekers fall into the trap of trying to think their way to inner peace. They think that the secret lies with someone else—a spiritual teacher or other holy person—and if they simply study with them long enough, they'll learn the answer to inner peace from them. We take a similar approach to resolving our inner conflicts and fears. Basically we have been taught to figure out God in our heads rather than experience God in our being. Think about it: We try to figure out our issues at the core of our negative inner dialogue with the same unconscious mind-set that created the negative dialogue in the first place. We replay the unconsciousness to only create more unconsciousness. In that state of mind, we are unstable, insecure, unconfident, and distracted, and we don't realize it. It is only when we bring in stillness with the intention to connect with God's spiritual energy that we have a true perspective of reality.

We all have the ability to experience inner peace for ourselves. It involves committing ourselves to action—not simply thinking.

So the first action is getting to the place where God is—in the present. Many of us have been led to believe that God is "out there" somewhere. We believe it because we haven't yet truly experienced his presence. Too many of us don't believe that it is possible to have that personal relationship with God. But once we access the peace of the present moment and experience God stop our fear and transform our pain, remove our stress, anxiety, and lack of self-esteem, we know that God isn't "out there" but within us every day.

It's All in the Questions

Most Christians truly believe that God reveals himself to us in our everyday life. He does! The problem is, they can't name very many times when they've actually had that experience. So how does it happen and when does it happen? We will never truly know that until we experience it in the present moment. The experience of our vibrant inner life changes our perspective of reality and our connectedness with Spirit. It grounds us in the peace of the present moment. And then whatever we thought was so important loses its urgency. We know what is primary, what is reality.

We might think to ourselves, "Am I practicing presence the right way? Am I practicing presence the wrong way?" But those are not the right questions. There are only three questions we have to ask:

1. Am I at peace now and do I know why?

2. If I am not at peace, do I know why?

3. And most important: If I am not at peace, do I know how to get back to peace?

If we can answer those three questions through our own experience, nothing else matters. We are free. We have allowed God's Spirit through the peace of the present moment to free us. And we spend every day proving that again and again to ourselves through the practice of presence. That's why we're never going back to the way we lived before.

MAKING MEANING OF THE MESSAGE

Inner conditioning is at the heart of practicing presence. Without doing it consistently, to start the day and throughout the day, we will not have confidence in it. It is our inner experience of calm and peace as we bring in stillness that keeps us returning to the present moment. In other words, it is the practice that teaches us or, I should say, it is the practice of bringing in stillness that allows God to teach us. As Jesus said in John 6:45, "They shall all be taught by God" (RSVCE). We all want God to reveal himself to us and teach us in our daily lives. But we have to remember, God's Spirit is always in the present moment and unfortunately most of us are rarely in the present moment. Inner-conditioning ourselves through the practice of presence keeps us close to the space where God can teach us: the always accessible present moment where he resides. And through his grace we have a choice.

SET THE INTENTION

Father, I pray that your peace keeps me close to the present moment so that you can teach me your ways.

PRACTICE PRESENCE

Bring in stillness and ask yourself the three questions to gauge your progress:

- Am I present now?

- How do I feel inside?

- Do I have a sense of peace within at some level?

See pages 10–11 for the details of this exercise or use the *Practicing Presence* app.

6

Resistance

Our Main Obstacle to True Peace

Suffering is the space between what I want and what is real.
—Anthony de Mello

We had a young sales representative working for us for about six months. He was very knowledgeable about our product, and he presented himself very well. But I began to notice that his performance wasn't consistent. I called him into my office one day to discuss it and to try to figure out what he might be doing wrong. We were talking about the process of how we present our product to doctors and therapists and how we follow up. As I asked him the questions, he kept responding to me by saying, "Yes, I know that." After he gave me that response several times, I stopped him, and I told him I hadn't asked if he *knew that*. I asked if he was *doing that*. He didn't know how to respond because he obviously wasn't doing that.

The problem was that he knew what he needed to do but he wasn't following through in his actions. He was resisting the steps he needed to take to achieve consistent success from his efforts.

It's the same for so many of us in our everyday lives. Every day we know there are certain things we need to do that are our responsibilities—big and small—and when we resist doing them, we create stress and anxiety for ourselves. Let's look at something as simple as taking out the trash. We can create stress for ourselves when we resist doing it. We wait and wait. We think about it and all the reasons we don't want to do it. We wait some more until it builds up to the point where we have to take care of it—right now! Once we've taken out the trash, we acknowledge how easy it was and wonder why we created such anxiety over such a simple thing.

This is also true about the more complicated, difficult situations we face in our lives. Often when confronted with a crisis in our personal life, our family life, or our professional life, instead of actually looking directly at the issue and trying to resolve it, we resist it, maybe even deny the crisis exists, and put off dealing with it—and put it off and put it off. Meanwhile we're building this negative cycle of anxiety, stress, and worry around the crisis, and eventually it affects our self-esteem.

So many of us are in resistance so often that we simply do not realize it or the pain it causes. Our resistance is killing us. So where do we get the strength to stop holding back?

What Is Resistance?

Resistance is the negative energy we put into what is happening in our life situation instead of accepting what is. It comes in many forms, both mental and physical, and they are all ways that we deny reality.

Our judgments and resentments are two pervasive forms of resistance to reality. We often form judgments about others as a way of coping with our shortcomings—pointing out a person's selfishness as a way of concealing our own selfish behaviors, for example, or refusing to acknowledge a person's skills or talents for fear of devaluing our own.

Denial, particularly in the face of criticism, is another form of resistance. Greg, one of my managers, disrespected a coworker. Deep down he knew his actions were wrong, but when he was confronted about it, he refused to admit any wrongdoing on his part. Instead of just acknowledging and apologizing for his bad behavior, he let the unease concerning the truth of his actions build up inside of him, causing him anxiety, stress, and shame.

Nonaction is a form of physical resistance. We all know of actions we can take to improve our lives, such as adopting an exercise program, stopping eating certain foods, or, like the manager, following a prescribed set of procedures at work. And yet we don't do them and make excuses for all the reasons why. Or we might start out strong, committing ourselves to an action and feeling the benefits. But after a week or two, when we've forgotten how bad we felt before we started the program or stopped eating those certain foods, we fall back into our old habits.

Resistance shows up in our relationships, our personal and professional lives, our finances, our self-esteem issues, and our connection with God. It provokes misery and suffering in our lives because when we resist what is, we accept what is not. It is a dysfunctional response to reality.

Spiritual teacher Eckhart Tolle describes this resistance as "missing the now."

If you continuously miss the now—resist it, dislike it, try to get away from it, reduce it to a means to an end, then you miss the essence of your life, and you are stuck in a dream world of images, concepts, labels, interpretations, judgments—the conditioned content of your mind that you take to be "yourself." And so you are disconnected from the fullness of life that is the "suchness" of this moment. When you are out of alignment with what is, you are out of alignment with life.[1]

Resistance is a powerful force, yet we often don't recognize it. We just assume it is natural. Fifteen or twenty years ago, I was an in-control person, and I thought my business, my friends, my lifestyle, my relationships with my wife and kids all seemed perfect—right up until it didn't work anymore. I found myself overcome with self-doubt. I felt like I was a user, using the circumstances in my life to enhance my own sense of self. I don't know where these feelings of self-doubt came from, but they hit me right between the eyes. How could everything be so good and yet I felt so bad and so lacking? I was finally ready to acknowledge my own resistance, to face my own selfishness and insecurity.

We begin to recognize how truly destructive resistance is to our inner well-being and peace when our awareness starts to change and we begin to feel the effects of it in our own body. Tense muscles, a clenched jaw, a tight and nervous stomach are all physical signs of inner distress. To ignore such physical symptoms is yet another form of resistance.

For me, the will to stop the resistance, to accept reality and face it, came through the practice of presence. It allowed me to see clearly the misery I was causing myself and sometimes others. Only the practice of presence put resistance in perspective and gave me the strength I did not think I had. As I stopped the resistance and faced my issues, it was like lifting a five-hundred-pound weight off my chest. I began to experience change from the inside out. In this state of surrender, nothing in this world has power over me because I am not lifting the burden by myself.

Confronting Resistance with Presence

The practice of presence helps to block our problems and life situations from taking over. It helps us avoid making instant judgments about people, situations, and ourselves, and it stops our resentments, which all ultimately cause us pain. It halts the comparisons—Are we better than or less than . . . ?—that we make so often we don't even realize we are doing it. It slowly dissolves our diminished self-esteem and decreases resistance to what is happening at this moment.

How does the practice of presence stop resistance? It puts us in the present moment, where we connect with God's Spirit within us. We become acutely aware of living our life rather than our life situation. All the ways we deceive ourselves drop away, and we trust in our sense of our true self. When we are consciously present in this moment, we can't have resentments toward anyone, we can't judge people, and we can't let anger take us over. There can be no jealousy or envy because all that kills our peace. God's Spirit lets us know that we cannot get away with negative intentions and gives us the courage to face anything because we know the consequences of living a false life. Our authentic self-esteem emerges from a deeper place, from our original self-esteem that we are and always have been beloved sons and daughters of God.

When you are not in the present moment, as Tolle explains, "you are struggling to reach a point in the future where there is greater security, aliveness, abundance, love, joy . . . unaware that those things make up the essence of who you are already. All that is required of you to have access to that essence is to make the present moment into your friend."[2]

I was giving a class on the practice of presence, and at the end, as I always do, I concluded with a round of Q&A. One gentleman raised his hand and asked me, "Well, presence doesn't change the problems that we have, does it?"

"No," I replied, "it doesn't change the problems that we have."

He smirked, revealing his doubt and distrust in the practice. I explained to him, "The real damage that our problems do to us is emotional. It's the intense anxiety, frustration, inner stress, and fears that we create by just dwelling on them over and over again. What the practice of presence does is stop us from allowing our problems to take us over emotionally: the primary cause of our inner conflicts and lack of self-esteem. It's not our problems but our reaction and resistance to our problems that cause us all the inner damage. Presence gives us a choice."

Why Do We Resist Practicing Presence?

So what stops us from embracing such a simple practice? What prevents us from letting go of our preconceived notions of how to deal with our stress and anxiety and finally try an exercise that gets to the heart of the matter? In essence, we fear change.

Vinita Hampton Wright, an author and practitioner of Ignatian spirituality, outlines four ways we resist letting go of old habits and beliefs, and I've adapted them as a way of exploring why we might resist practicing presence.[3]

First, letting go of old ways of coping with our problems can feel like failure. We may feel that our way of addressing our problems hasn't solved them yet, but if we hang in a little longer, it will. To change course now is to throw in the towel and admit defeat, to admit that the way we've been living isn't working or is wrong.

"The power of denial is so strong that we hold on to false beliefs, even if the evidence overwhelmingly points against it," writer Melissa Chu points out. "We do this partly because of our fear of change. We hold on to old things and refuse to let go, which clogs up space for new ideas, people, or opportunities. . . . The other reason behind our denial is the time investment involved. When we spend so much time and energy trying to make something work, it becomes harder to cut our losses and move on."[4]

Second, if we give up our existing ways of behaving and coping—if through the practice of presence we drop our judgments about who we are or aren't—what then? As Wright explains, detachment has the potential to leave a void. We may fear losing touch with who we are, of losing the foundation of our identity, even if that identity—who we think we are—is rooted in pain.

As life coach and self-help writer Connie Chapman acknowledges, clearing away old ways of being— no matter the suffering they may cause us—is humbling and can lead us to dig our heels in deeper to our existing ways of thinking.

"Clearing away of the old is necessary to create space and a clean slate to lay new foundations and build more authentic structures," Chapman explains. "Many of us struggle with letting go, as we fear the space that will be created and we have no idea who we are without these external forms that define us. This can be one of the most scary and unsettling times. When things in our life begin to crumble around us, it can trigger feelings of anxiety, grief, and the desire to cling."[5]

Third, we become comfortable and secure in what we know. Here we're ruled by the Irish proverb "Better the devil you know than the devil you don't know." Even though we suffer in our cycle of negative thinking and want to stop the self-defeating inner dialogue, it's a condition we are familiar with. In fact, some of us might interpret the constant rehashing of our problems as productivity. And again, we may wonder who we will be without the pain and suffering that have come to define our lives.

As Christian spiritual leader Rick Warren explains, "We say, 'It's just like me to be . . .' and 'It's just the way I am.' The unconscious worry is that if I let go of my habit, my hurt, or my hang-up, who will I be? This fear can definitely slow down your growth."[6]

Fourth, to practice presence means we have to face reality—to look at our problems for what they are—and most of us would rather deny those problems exist. Many of us may take comfort in the illusion that we're in control. When we practice presence, we surrender to the reality that we are led by God's Spirit; God is our teacher. The realization that it is not what we're doing, but what is being done to us shatters our illusion of control and puts us firmly in the hands of God.

As inspirational writer Rebecca Barlow Jordan explains, "To combat resistance requires change and change is hard. Some attitudes, even harmful ones if we let them, can settle like cement into our lives. And nothing short of God's blasting intervention can break them up and establish new ones."[7]

In the end, it is our ego that will try time and again to give us reasons why we cannot practice presence. For example, we resist practicing presence when we find ourselves saying, "I don't have time," "I'm too busy," "I'll do it later," or "I don't need to practice presence."

I ran into my friend Rachel at the grocery store. She had attended some of my talks on practicing presence, and I knew that at one point she was serious about her practice. I asked her how it was going.

"Life took over," she said, throwing her hands up in exasperation. "With everything going on, all the pressures I have with family and work and the church fundraising, my head was spinning. I was just too stressed. It's just too hard, and I felt like a failure."

"You don't have time to take three conscious breaths in a row throughout the day, in order to access God's spiritual energy?" I asked her. "That's your ego winning out. First of all, we breathe all day long—all we're talking about is being aware of those breaths. And second, while we are breathing, no matter how many breaths we're taking, we're enhancing our inner well-being by shutting down the internal negative dialogue—the kind of stuff you're feeling right now, all the compulsive thinking. When we actually do it and experience how different we feel inside, we tap into its lasting power."

"You're right," Rachel said. "I know how much it helped me when I was breathing throughout the day.

I'm going to be more consistent." Then she said, "Let me know when you are giving another presence talk. I want to come with my husband."

Jesus tells us to enter through the narrow gate that leads to life (Matthew 7:13–14). But our problem is all our resistances have us running around in circles looking for that gate. Stillness allows us to see the gate, to know where it is. When we practice presence, we realize our capacity to open the gate. And as we become consciously present, we go through the gate. Once through, there is an unmistakable contrast, an alternative to our inner chaos. The inner negative dialogue has stopped. There is no anxiety, stress, worry, or lack of self-esteem. When we compare that to being unconscious, living through memory or anticipation, or being in resistance to what is happening at this moment—what's on the other side of the gate—we will always have time to choose presence.

It's Not Difficult

I can explain the negative effects of resistance, and what I say may be very compelling and almost everyone would agree with me, but very few people will really change on words alone. Words alone will not convince most people, just like words did not convince me.

There has to be a change in our awareness of our vibrant inner life and the damage our resistance does to it. We have to know through our own personal experience that there is an alternative to how we feel in a state of anxiety, a state of resistance, and how painful it can be at times. We have to experience what it feels like to have the power to actually face our issues, that inner confidence. It is only through our personal experience that we are convinced of the power of the present moment.

Every day we are awake for approximately one thousand minutes. Taking three conscious breaths throughout the day to access God's spiritual energy takes no time at all. It doesn't require any special equipment, it doesn't interfere with our surroundings, and it can be done anywhere. It becomes effortless as we inner-condition ourselves because we want to come back to the inner freedom and connectedness we experience inside.

While special equipment isn't required, we can use easily accessible technology to help us get started and stay on track. Some people have said to me, "Trying to take three conscious breaths throughout the day, I get busy and I just forget." So I tell them that there is a very simple fix for that—we need only set the reminder app on our smartphone to prompt us (see page 121). So even if we're busy and forget, we always have our phones reminding us, "Okay, now go back to creating space, using our breath to bring in stillness."

Because I have made practicing presence primary in my life for the last fifteen years, it's pretty automatic for me. But I decided to try setting the reminder on my phone. And I was very surprised that as automatic as it has become to me to take many conscious breaths throughout the day, the reminder deepens the practice and makes it even more powerful. So in response I created the *Practicing Presence—A Christian Way* app, which has a programmable reminder feature and is intended to be used as a companion to this book. It makes something that was very good even better. Using the app serves as a consistent reminder that we have a choice not to be taken over by negative emotions and reactions throughout the day as different life situations pop up unexpectedly.

Through the practice of presence, we consciously and intentionally start to have a relationship with our vibrant inner life, and that is when we really start to experience the power of God's spiritual energy within us.

Through continuous practice, we condition ourselves to become aware of the constant flow of thoughts and the inner negative response, which allows us to see how useless all the compulsive and repetitive thinking is, which aids us in letting go of our resistance. It grounds us and balances us, and we are able to connect with the goodness that is already within us. We are never as stable or happy as we are when present to God's Spirit within us.

Some people have said to me that practicing presence sounds ridiculously simple. And they're correct! God made it that way because he knows that most of us are ridiculously unconscious. If we don't believe in Spirit, then how do we explain the moments of unconditional love we have had and what we experience inside? Where did the peace, joy, and contentment come from? Not us. It flows through the stillness as our resistance stops. Once we have experienced the power of Spirit within ourselves, can anyone tell us that it is wrong or that it's not real? Absolutely not! It is then that we start to know. We go from believing to knowing and on our way to peace.

MAKING MEANING OF THE MESSAGE

Resistance is one of the biggest obstacles to our peace of mind and to practicing presence. When we resist what is, we are accepting a false reality that we have created in our ego mind. As we practice presence, that becomes very clear to us. What we resist has power over us, but what we accept in nonresistance no longer has power over us. Nonresistance and acceptance free us from the inside so we are experiencing our true life now rather than reacting negatively to our life situations—all the things happening around our life in our relationships, in the work we do, financial worries, our security, our inner well-being. Then we can have the confidence to deal with them all. But when we dwell on them or obsess over them again and again in resistance, we have taken ourselves out of reality. All the things in our life situation—they come and they go. They are not permanent. Our life is permanent, eternal, and it is whole, complete, and accessible always. In the practice of presence we have an alternative, a contrast: Are we going to create our inner fears and conflicts or accept the peace of the present moment? Nothing in our life situation is as powerful as that peace.

SET THE INTENTION

Father, allow your peace to stop the resistance I put in my daily life and change that resistance to acceptance of what is happening at this moment.

PRACTICE PRESENCE

Bring in stillness and ask yourself the three questions to gauge your progress:

- Am I present now?

- How do I feel inside?

- Do I have a sense of peace within at some level?

See pages 10–11 for the details of this exercise or use the *Practicing Presence* app.

≈ 7 ≈

The Courage to Stop Negative Thinking and Gossip

The Awareness That We Take Our Life Situations and Turn Them into Problems

Unhappiness or negativity is a disease on our planet. What pollution is on the outer level is negativity on the inner. It is everywhere, not just in places where people don't have enough, but even more so where they have more than enough.

—Eckhart Tolle

A woman came up to me after a talk I gave and explained to me that she is the caregiver for her mother and their relationship had become difficult. She told me that she is with her mother most of the day, taking care of her needs, but that her mother often says hurtful things and seems unappreciative of her daughter's efforts.

"She makes me feel guilty about the whole situation, as if I'm doing something wrong," the woman shared with me. "Even when I'm not with her, I really can't stop thinking about it. It's on my mind all the time. There's so much stress. Why can't I get past this and recognize what's most important in life?"

We've all been where this woman is. When faced with a challenging situation, we try to think our way out of it. We believe if we replay the difficult conversation in our minds one more time, we'll find the answer to the problem. Or if we rehash the scenario one more time, imagining all the possible outcomes, we'll ease our anxiety and get on with our life.

But when we get stuck in the cycle of compulsive thinking, we're not actually living our life. Instead we're living our life situation, dwelling on something that has already happened or worrying about what might happen in the future. How can we focus on what's real now if we're so often mentally somewhere else?

Until we have the courage and confidence to stop negative thinking, we're just going to keep missing our lives and the most important things in them. It is only when we are still and experience the peace of the present moment that life opens up to us and we experience true peace.

What Does It Mean to Stop Negative Thinking?

We've been conditioned to believe that a mind in motion is a productive mind. If our mind is busy, we must be working on a solution. Or we may think that if we do not constantly dwell on a problem or issue we have, we don't care about it. In some ways a busy mind gives us a sense that we're in control. But just because our minds are swirling with activity doesn't mean they are being useful. Consider the common expression "like a chicken running around with its head cut off." Motion is not the same as meaningful action. The senseless busyness of compulsive thinking stirs our emotions, creating more anxiety, frustration, and inner fear, and is often the cause of our suffering. The more we dwell, the less effective we are and the more misery we create—"we" become the problem because we have made the problem personal. All problems are life situations that we turn into problems.

Another term for compulsive thinking is *thought chatter*. Thought chatter—voluntary or involuntary—is mental activity that includes reliving past situations, reactions, and behaviors in a fruitless, tiring loop. While thought chatter can include positive daydreaming, more often it is a negative inner conversation that spins us into a damaging alternate reality. Spiritual teacher Steve Taylor describes this mental noise as "a psychological aberration, a kind of quirk of the mind."

> Thought-chatter . . . creates a barrier between us and our experience. It stops us experiencing the world in an immediate way. It creates a fog of abstraction in our minds, which dilutes and obscures all our experience, everything we see, hear, smell, feel, or touch, so that reality becomes a shadow. It may even create a sense of unreality, when the memories, images, and scenarios that run through our mind appear more real than our actual experience."[1]

In essence, the biggest impediment to our peace of mind is our own thoughts. We are a society addicted to thinking—particularly negative thinking. It is the elephant in the room that no one mentions, because we do not realize we are doing it until it takes us over. Our compulsive thinking lifts us completely out of the present moment.

Negative Thinking by Another Name: Gossip

At times we allow our own inner negativity to direct our actions, and we say things that are sometimes hurtful about family or friends—otherwise known as gossip. Gossip in any communal setting—the workplace, church, sports teams, school environments, volunteer organizations, and, of course, our families—is one of the more prominent and pervasive ways that we see our negative thinking play out in our lives, and it is a cancer. It not only stirs our own inner conflicts, fears, and insecurities, but it also creates a negative atmosphere in the external world around us. Like any other form of negative thinking, it prevents us from being able to stay in the present and connect with God's Spirit.

Merriam-Webster's dictionary defines *gossip* as "a rumor or report of an intimate nature." But that just skims the surface, doesn't it? Often when we gossip, we focus on the faults and failings of others. We rush to reveal what we know—or think we know—about others, and the more intimate, embarrassing, or shameful it seems, the more eager we are to share.

Gossip may seem that it is projected at other people, but in fact, it reflects our own inner lives. First, we unconsciously aim to put others down so that we can raise ourselves up. It is a human compulsion to measure ourselves against others, and there are countless motivations for this, such as jealousy, envy, desire, greed, and, perhaps most commonly, insecurity and lack of self-confidence. When Jake tells his coworkers about Bill's weak presentation at the conference last week, he is attempting to bolster his confidence about his own job performance. When Tammy describes Jill's struggle with a new exercise program to other members of the class, she's hoping to convince the others—and herself—of her fitness superiority. As Eckhart Tolle explains in *A New Earth*:

> "Why do you see the speck that is in your brother's eye, but do not notice the log that is in your own eye?" In the Bible, Jesus's question remains unanswered, but the answer is, of course, "Because when I criticize or condemn another, it makes me feel bigger, superior."[2]

Second, when we know something that other people don't know, it makes us feel special. As sociologists Jack Levin and Arnold Arluke explain in their book *Gossip: The Inside Scoop*, gossip is having the "inside scoop.... *Inside* means only certain people—the insiders—have been granted the privilege of passing on a 'juicy morsel' or a 'shocking revelation.'"[3] It is human nature to want to be included. And being the privileged bearer of "news" also gives us a sense of power and control—we get to decide who we share the information with and when.

Third, sometimes we simply want to entertain. We want attention turned toward us. As I mentioned earlier, as humans we all want to feel good about ourselves, to have high self-esteem, to have meaning in our lives, and to be loved. When people want to be near us and listen to what we have to say, we feel loved.

But what we are doing when we are gossiping, or what Paul describes in Romans as "whispering," is the opposite of giving love. When we play out our negative thinking in this way, we are harming others and ourselves. As it says in Proverbs, "The words of a talebearer [a gossiper] are as wounds, and they go down into the innermost parts of the belly" (18:8 KJV). Any relief we feel from the burdens of our inner conflicts, insecurities, and fear that is achieved by talking about other people's mistakes or shortcomings is only temporary. The negativity we breed in ourselves and in everyone around us by gossiping can be long-lasting and destructive.

The Desert Fathers and Mothers often warned against *murmuring*, the word they used to describe complaining but also gossiping. They saw murmuring as a barrier to our vibrant inner life—which we experience when we're present.

> When malice takes control, we can easily justify a few words of gossip or complaining here and there. Soon a pattern develops that competes with our openness to the Spirit that will eat away at the foundation of our spiritual life.[4]

Like other forms for negative thinking, gossiping is an obstacle to presence for two primary reasons: gossip focuses on the past or anticipates the future, and gossip makes us believe our insecurities need only be managed rather than overcome. This means there is always some degree of distraction created from the suffering we experience as a result of our low self-esteem. An example of that is Jake, who gossiped about Bill's poor presentation at a conference in order to build up his confidence. Jake likely perceived that his listeners agreed with him, which made Jake feel better about his own work performance and temporarily neutralized any threat Jake may have felt from Bill in the workplace. Sure, Jake's self-confidence improved and his insecurities were quieted—but not for long. Once he was back at home, alone with himself and away from his listeners, those insecurities came back. In fact, they were now compounded by shame because he knew that bad-mouthing Bill wasn't the right thing to do.

The distraction of his insecurities kept Jake trapped in a cycle outside of reality, and it didn't make him feel good. In order to break that cycle, he had to change—not manage through gossip—how he felt inside. To alter how we feel inside and grow spiritually takes time and practice, and first we must believe it's possible. When we're present to God's spiritual energy within us, we have the confidence to change because we are not doing it on our own. We are challenged to connect with our vibrant inner life, God's Spirit within us where our courage lies. When we allow him to guide us, our insecurities start to dissolve along with our guilt and shame.

Breaking the Cycle

In order for us to get out from under the control of our negative thinking, our thought chatter, we need to slow it down—or as I like to say, we need to stop thinking. When we practice presence, we break that negative cycle of thought, emotion, and reaction that causes so much of our guilt, anxiety, and fear. When we bring in stillness, the controlling power is shifted from our thought chatter to our vibrant inner life, God's Spirit within us. We gain a true perspective of what's really happening around us. In the clarity of the present moment, we see our life challenges for what they are untangled from our emotions and can make clear decisions based on reality.

Spiritual teacher Eckhart Tolle calls this dis-identifying with our thinking mind:

When we are identified with our thinking mind, our experience of life is constricted and limited to an opaque screen of words, images, concepts, and labels—second-hand representations of life that might as well be a movie on a screen. When you create even a momentary gap in the incessant thinking and chatter taking place in your mind, the light of your consciousness grows stronger. The world around you becomes more vibrant and real. Your experience of life is direct and alive, you are present in your experience, and thus you are able to touch life directly.[5]

Before I began practicing presence, I would sometimes find myself with family or friends, having dinner, watching TV, or at an event, and yet I was not really there. My mind was running, thinking of all the different things that had nothing to do with what was happening at that moment, and not knowing why. It was distracting, exhausting, and anxiety-producing.

With the practice of presence bringing in stillness, my awareness has changed, which includes my awareness of others. It allows me to become a better listener and more in tune with how others are feeling, because I know how to stop the distractions of my own inner resentments, instant judgments, and fear. When I am present to God's Spirit within me, I am also fully present to those around me.

Perfection Isn't Possible

As Taylor points out, it is unlikely that we will ever be able to entirely stop our thought chatter. What we can do, however, is quit allowing our negative emotional reactions to take over. It is only through consistent practice, bringing in stillness many times throughout the day, that we keep in touch with our vibrant inner life; the practice is what teaches and inner-conditions us. And while the calm and peace we experience in this moment are not permanent—we keep renewing them throughout the day—the more we experience them, the greater our confidence that we have access to them and know how to return to them.

I was talking to a friend and I told her that practicing presence stops our inner negative dialogue by 90 percent.

"Yes," she replied, "but we still have anxiety and stress."

I said, "Let me give you an example. Let's say you have a very painful back problem that interferes with every aspect of your life because it is so uncomfortable and painful. You go to the doctor and he says, 'Look, here is what I want you to do. I want you to do this stretching exercise three times an hour, for twenty seconds each time, and it should dramatically help your pain.' You try the exercise as directed and after a short period of time your pain is eased by 90 percent. It doesn't stop the pain entirely, but it no longer interferes with any part of your life and causes you no uncomfortable issues. Would you continue with the exercise or would you stop it because it didn't get you 100 percent pain-free?"

"Of course," she said. "I would definitely continue with the exercise."

Practicing presence is like the effective stretching exercise. Bringing stillness into our lives reduces our negative thought chatter to the degree that it doesn't stir up the negative emotions to cloud us from reality and cause us pain. But the key is in the practice. No practice, no stillness. No stillness, no peace.

Thinking versus Doing

One day, as I was leading a class on practicing presence, a man kept interrupting me to ask questions. It was obvious he was trying to figure out the answer to presence, the answer to his problems. He wasn't interested in bringing in stillness in his life, and practicing presence either first thing in the morning or throughout the day just wasn't something he thought he could do. He just wanted me to tell him a nugget of wisdom that would bring him instant and lasting peace—and that simply doesn't exist.

As this person asked yet another question, I quoted Albert Einstein: "You cannot solve a problem with the same consciousness that created it." Then I told him, "You're looking for an answer but it's not an answer; it's an action." Most of us begin the search for a solution to our dis-ease just as this person was doing, by seeking answers, gathering information, and analyzing the problem or scenario. We sign up for classes and workshops, we buy books, we seek out the advice of our favorite teachers. Yet despite our best efforts, more information or knowledge does not change our consciousness, and too often it energizes our ego.

Many of us have a similar approach to religion and experiencing presence—we get so focused on the readings and rituals of religion that we don't make time to encounter God in our own lives. Reverend Jim Burklo, the associate dean of religious life at the University of Southern California, writes about getting to know Fr. Thomas Hand, an American Jesuit priest who spent many years practicing Zen Buddhism. Burklo writes,

> Father Hand once said that the Catholic Church had it backwards on the education of its lay people. "We

teach them doctrine and dogma for years, and then, maybe, possibly, if we get around to it, we teach them how to experience God. What we need to do is teach them to experience God first, and then that will make sense or nonsense of the doctrine and dogma."[6]

Burklo describes a similar experience in his upbringing in the mainline liberal Protestant Christian tradition. "We memorized scripture, we learned about church history, we read Bible stories. But experiencing God directly? Not once from birth through my teenage and young adult years did I ever get any introduction to spiritual practice or mysticism in church."[7] Burklo yearned to *know* God, not just know about God.

"Be still, and know that I am God," we learn in Psalm 46:10. The solution to our suffering doesn't come through answers but through experience—through knowing. Stillness comes not through thought but through awareness. Once we internalize awareness through experience, everything changes, and then we are truly being led by God's Spirit within us. As Jesuit theologian Karl Rahner said, "If [we as Christians do] not experience something, [we] will be nothing."[8]

To achieve this awareness, we must consciously start to have a relationship with our vibrant inner life, and this is done through bringing in stillness throughout the day through practicing presence. We may start by incorporating three intentional breaths every hour—or more—throughout the day, but the ultimate goal is making conscious breathing a habit.

I asked my friend Frank if he was practicing presence by conscious breathing throughout the day. He said, "Yes, you know, when I get really anxious, I start breathing."

"Does it help you?" I asked.

"Yes," he said, but I could see that it wasn't helping him very much.

I explained to Frank that the reason we aim to have a consistent breathing practice throughout the day is to keep us close to the present moment. I compared the experience to driving a car.

"You can't expect the practice of presence to be effective if you only practice it when you feel stressed out. It should be done no matter what your mood is. If your mood is good, it will make it better. If you're anxious and stressed, it will get you out of your negative mind-set. By staying close to the present moment, you make it much easier for yourself to get back to reality.

"Imagine you're in a car driving at ten miles an hour, and you go around a bend only to see that there's something right in front of you. You put on your brakes, and you're easily able to slow down in time to avoid an accident. Now imagine you're in a car driving fifty miles an hour, you make that turn, and there's something right in front of you. Guess what? You're going to run smack into that obstruction, and you're going to cause damage.

"It's the same thing with our mind. If we give it all that negative energy, it just takes off at a pace we can't stop and we're constantly crashing into our inner fears and anxieties. We're so wrapped up in our negative spin that getting back to presence becomes much more difficult. But if we stay close to the present moment—if we keep to ten miles per hour—getting back to presence is not very difficult. It's quick and easy. We continuously stay within reach of our vibrant inner life and its stillness is always accessible."

As I explained to Frank, by staying close to the present moment we can't hold resentments toward anyone, we can't judge people or ourselves, we can't let anger take us over, and we can't compare ourselves to anyone. When we're present to God's Spirit within us, it is impossible to have a lack of self-esteem. When we practice regularly, we know this through our own experiences and we put our trust in the power of the present moment.

Words will not convince us. It is only our personal experience of God's presence that changes us in a lasting way. Spiritual leader Richard Rohr says overriding our modern DIY mind-set with this trusting mind-set is admittedly not easy:

> Scripture clearly says, in many ways, that God helps those who *trust in* God, not those who help themselves. We need to be told that very strongly because of our "do it yourself" orientation. . . . It takes applying the brakes, letting go of our own plans, allowing Another, and experiencing power from a Larger Source to really move to higher awareness. Otherwise, there is no real transformation.[9]

Switching from a thinking mind-set to an action mind-set takes discipline and commitment, for sure. Fortunately the practice of presence forgives us our human failings and doesn't require perfection.

I explained this to Anne when I ran into her at a community event. Anne had been very committed to practicing presence. She did the simple practices first thing in the morning and followed through with them throughout the day. At the time, she acknowledged that her stress and anxiety levels were greatly reduced. I didn't see her for about six months, until I bumped into her at the community gathering, and I could clearly see that she was very unpresent. So I asked her if she was still doing the practices.

"A little bit," she said, "but not as much as I was before."

"Do you remember what you told me, about how much better you felt inside when you actually did the practices?" I asked her.

"Yes," she said, "but my son has started college and he's had some problems, and my husband has changed jobs, so it's been really hectic. It seems as if there's a new problem popping up every day."

"That's all the more reason to practice," I encouraged her. "Do you really think you're going to face all these obstacles and distractions in your life feeling alone and isolated? Sometimes we get out of the practice of presence and we lose the confidence we had in it to connect us to God's healing presence and put our lives in true perspective. We don't think we can get back to where we were. But that's completely false. Not only will we be able to get back to where we were, but we'll be on an even deeper level. Once we come back and breakthrough, the reminder of the power of presence is that much greater. Every time we come consciously into the presence moment it is a new beginning."

I saw Anne a few months later at a mutual friend's birthday party. I didn't have to ask her how she was doing. She came up to me and said, "I'm practicing presence consistently and you were right. Now I can almost stop my racing mind and worrying almost immediately."

"That's great!" I replied. "What's important to remember is that it's the peace and power of the present moment that is doing it."

Anywhere, Anytime but with Intention

I was reading about Carl Jung, the famous psychotherapist, who had a summer home in Switzerland. In that home he had a quiet room, and he said that when he was there, that was when he was the most at peace.

I had a similar experience. About twenty-five years ago, Patricia and I had a small cabin in the mountains. When I went there with my family for weekends, I always felt that it truly was the most peaceful place for me to be. I also have a number of friends who have their own special places where, when they are there, they feel different inside—there's more calm and peace in their lives.

As I started practicing presence on a daily basis throughout the day, I realized that it really didn't matter where I was; I didn't have to be in a special place to slow down my thought chatter and experience what I've come to know as the power of the present moment. I didn't have to be in our cabin in the mountains to feel that sense of peace. Wherever and whenever I took the time to bring in stillness, to quiet the negative inner dialogue, God's spiritual energy was there. The peace that comes through stillness is what God intended for us to experience always, no matter where we are or what our life situation is.

As I was describing this realization to my friend Dan, he said, "I know exactly what you mean. My wife and I go away to Hawaii for a couple weeks every year, and it's the only time we truly unwind and relax. No matter what happens over the months, we always make that trip a priority."

Dan's much-needed tropical time-out may be an important time of rest and recharge, but it's not the lasting experience of presence that I'm talking about. We might say we're going away, we're going to just chill out and relax, and we initially feel a sense of relief. But soon enough, all the inner negative dialogue comes back. It *is* a relief, but only for a short period of time. Stillness is the cure.

"Be still, and know that I am God." To *think* means to ponder, to consider in one's own mind. To *know* means to be certain of, to be aware; to have experienced or encountered. To know requires more than study and planning; it requires intention, commitment, and training—or what I call *inner-conditioning*. When we regularly practice presence, we know that we have access to God's Holy Spirit—that which gives us life, energy, and power—within us. Every time we breathe into this awareness with the right intention and become still, even if for only a few moments, we experience his peace at some level.

MAKING MEANING OF THE MESSAGE

How many times have we allowed our mind to literally run away with us and let all those negative thoughts take us over? Before making the practice of presence primary in my life, it must have happened to me a thousand times. And the worst part is, we don't know how it happens. It all begins in our unobserved mind because we are not in touch with how we feel inside. When I first started practicing presence, I can remember getting the feeling that if I stopped thinking, I was going to miss something—and I was right. What I was going to miss was all the misery I cause myself through all the compulsive and repetitive negative thinking I was doing when I was in an unconscious state. The practice of presence stops that negative cycle by making us aware of how our negative thinking may be playing out in our external world, such as when we gossip, which often creates turmoil all around us and creates a barrier to peace. The practice of presence also makes us aware of the unease building up inside, which often leads to inner chaos. Through the practice of consciously breathing throughout the day we bring ourselves back to the present moment, the only reality there is. And we then realize we have a choice. When we are in an unconscious state, living through memory or anticipation, that is a false reality we have created in our mind. In that state we do not realize we have a choice. That is how the practice of presence teaches us. As Eckhart Tolle says, it is a terrible affliction not to be able to stop our mind from thinking. The practice of presence gives us that choice.

SET THE INTENTION

Father, when I feel like I don't want to stop thinking, let me realize *that* is the most important time to stop thinking.

PRACTICE PRESENCE

Bring in stillness and ask yourself the three questions to gauge your progress:

- Am I present now?

- How do I feel inside?

- Do I have a sense of peace within at some level?

See pages 10–11 for the details of this exercise or use the *Practicing Presence* app.

∞ 8 ∞

We All Want Peace

The Practice of Presence Gets Us There

> *We recognize that peace (whether internal or external) is a grace. It is not something we achieve on our own, but rather something that we receive from the loving heart of God.*
>
> —Carl McColman

My wife, Patricia, and I were in New York, and she wanted to go to Times Square. We hadn't been there in a while, so I said okay. When we got there, the place was completely packed. I don't really like large crowds; I try to avoid them. And I just didn't feel like being there. I was a little impatient, a reflection of my own resistance to what was happening in the moment. So I started to practice presence by breathing—not just biologically but with the intention of connecting with my vibrant inner life. And within a minute or two I felt completely calm, even though there were literally hundreds of people all around me. I felt so good I just continued to breathe consciously. I went from feeling calm to having a deep sense of peace and joy within myself, which is God's spiritual energy inside me. It was like the crowd, the noise, the chaos of Times Square didn't matter. Instead of being impatient and annoyed with it, I was completely enjoying it. And I thought to myself, this is the power of presence—it brings us to peace.

What Is Peace?

To many of us, peace seems unattainable. We envision a steady state of bliss during which we're completely unaffected by conflict. We have no troubles, no enemies, no stress, no pressure. This is what I describe as *worldly peace*, an ego-driven concept that leads us to try to manipulate the external conditions around us so that we can get what we want for ourselves. And we often go after this kind of peace in worldly ways. We think, "If I do these things right, if I have these things, if I have her or his approval, if I put myself in this environment, if I achieve this level of success, then I'll be happy, I'll be at peace." We try to manufacture peace through discipline and willpower, by way of our own creation and control.

The practice of presence, however, leads us to a different kind of peace, *the peace of God*, an experience that is often difficult to explain. The apostle Paul described it as the "peace that no one can completely understand" (Philippians 4:7 CEV). The German theologian Rudolf Otto applied the term *numinous* to describe "this 'extra' in the meaning of 'holy' above and beyond the meaning of goodness" that might be experienced as God's peace.[1] Carl Jung later frequently used the term *numinous* to describe what I call the peace of God and what he described as an experience that feeds "the hunger of the soul."[2] He believed that encounters with the numinous could cause major transformations.[3]

Reliance on the peace and power of God's spiritual energy for most Christians has largely been lost. In the Acts of the Apostles, letters, and epistles written after Pentecost it was the foundation of the church, which changed the world. The power of God's Spirit was constantly referred to in practical daily life as the energy source for all that is good, with the power to change each of us from the inside by stopping our fear and transforming our pain. This obviously happened because they were experiencing that power!

Why have we stopped teaching how to access this most powerful gift from God? Jesus's Spirit is as accessible and vibrant today as it was on Pentecost. It appears we have abandoned it. This does not have to be! Whatever we call it, we know the experience of God's peace as more powerful than anything we've ever experienced before. It's when we know we are present to the eternal. And when we tap into that source, we know we are connected to everyone and everything around us. We know we're not alone.

As spiritual teacher Carl McColman explains, this kind of peace isn't so much about feelings, which are conditional and fleeting, or about avoiding problems, as it is about an awareness of our relationship with God.

> This peace . . . is more about an equipoise that finds inner reliance on God. Such reliance knows God to be a rock that enables us to place our trust in God, enabling us to be present even in the midst of the pain and suffering that seems so overwhelming. Being rooted in God doesn't make pain, suffering, dread, anger, and other powerful feelings and states of mind go away. But it does offer a new perspective, a higher

vantage point that can enable us to remember that even the fiercest suffering and most egregious injustice is never the final word.[4]

Worldly peace, for the most part, is mind-made, and it is temporary. Ask anyone how they're doing and they're likely to say, "I feel good. I feel okay. I feel fine." But along with that, whether it's said or unsaid, there are also times of the day when they're also going to feel anxious, uneasy, stressed out, or not very good about themselves. All of us experience this. We've also all experienced that false happiness being exposed for the reality it is: an ego assumption that always crashes.

God's peace is eternal not because we're permanently calm and without conflicts in our life, but because God's peace is always there, at the core of our vibrant inner life, available for us if we only allow ourselves to become aware of it. Jesus himself describes this in the parable of the hidden treasure in Matthew 13:44. The man finds the treasure, buries it, sells all his possessions, and purchases the field in which it is buried. The man doesn't need to carry the treasure around all the time to know its worth; he can go back to it whenever he wants to be refreshed by its value and beauty. Each of us is that field and buried within each of us is the treasure of God's spiritual energy. It's through the practice of presence that we know what we're looking for—awareness of God's presence—and we know how to find it—through the stillness that allows us to experience our vibrant inner life again and again.

Whenever I do jail ministry, before the actual service I always give a talk on being present to God's spiritual energy within us and all around us. One day I had a small group of four men, and I asked each of them to think of a time or an experience in their life when they felt a real sense of peace, inner freedom, and inner happiness. I gave them about a minute, and then I asked each one individually to share their answer. The last inmate who gave me an answer was an older guy around sixty. He told me that years ago he was driving to work early in the morning, and he was going over a bridge. As he crossed the bridge, he noticed how beautiful the lake was below and the hills that were all around him. The sun was just starting to rise, and he said it was so beautiful and peaceful that, once he got over the bridge, he pulled off to the side of the road and just sat in awe of it. As he told this story, he was like a different person, just reliving that experience of true peace he had experienced years ago.

I said to him, "As beautiful as that setting was—the lake, the hills, the sun rising that just sort of stopped you in your tracks—all of that natural beauty did not create what you felt inside. What actually happened to you—and what happens to all of us—is that all that beauty made it easier for you to become still inside, and through that stillness you were able to access that intense peace and happiness that's in you all the time. Every time that you bring in stillness and connect with your vibrant inner life, God's Spirit within you, you will experience that peace."

Peace in Motion

It's important for us to remember that bringing in stillness doesn't mean stopping—we don't have to halt our everyday activities to feel the benefits of the practice of presence and tap into peace. And this applies to activities both physical and mental. Take discernment, for example—it's an action we all engage to various degrees throughout our lives and can be, for many of us, a time of great pain, often self-induced.

Discernment to me is not just about making a decision. It's about my spiritual response to what is happening in my life. I can remember a time when I had a difficult decision to make in my business. It literally consumed me for a couple of weeks. It just kept popping up in my mind—I was going over it and over it, which I normally don't do, but it was really quite anxiety-producing. What that experience taught me was that even though the decision-making process was anxiety-producing, through the practice of presence I had a sense of peace around the problem. The problem didn't take me over with negative emotions and negative reactions. It was upsetting, but by staying in reality and not having resistance to reality or the process of discernment, and especially the peace around it, the anxiety was neutralized. I was just *facing* a problem, and by practicing presence, I didn't *become* the problem through my unconsciousness in trying to deal with it.

Even in discernment we can bring in stillness. Without stillness we won't see reality clearly because we tend to be led by our ego energy when we are unconscious. Our ego can only make discernment more difficult, muddying our mind's clarity with thoughts of the past or projections of the future. And if we're not in the present moment, there can be no peace; we're not connected to God's spiritual energy. Stillness grounds us in the reality of this moment, the only reality there is, where we can make good decisions and where we can experience God's peace.

When we practice presence, we have moments of calm, serenity, and love that stop us in our tracks throughout the day and give us an instant change in our perspective of life now and how powerful the experience of God's spiritual energy really is. And most important, we know the source of it, and we know how to access the power of God's spiritual energy within us. It is through that experience that our whole life changes because anxiety, stress, worry, and lack of self-esteem no longer have power over us. True life now, in this moment, has broken through, and that experience cannot be duplicated by anything in this world.

Why Do We Resist Peace?

In John 14:27, Jesus tells us, "I give you peace, the kind of peace that only I can give. It isn't like the peace that this world can give. So don't be worried or afraid" (CEV).

Why would we resist the very thing all of us so badly want in our lives? In a nutshell, God's peace isn't something we can control or create, which in our ego-dominated unconsciousness makes us uncomfortable. When we acknowledge that we're not in control, we stoke our fears of being left out, missing something, or losing something. And we are emotionally immature at times because we're lost in all the compulsive and repetitive thinking. In that state, it is easier for us to chase a false peace that ultimately turns to misery at some level because it is not real or sustainable. It is the unconsciousness that makes it seem so hard to access peace.

In *The Power of Now*, Eckhart Tolle tells us that "love, joy, and peace cannot flourish until [we] have freed [ourselves] from mind dominance."[5] That's where the practice of presence comes in. When we are consciously present with the intention of connecting with God's peace inside and all around us, we find that there is very little or no resistance because our ego energy has no power over us in the present moment. But we must have confidence in the practice to truly know that peace is available at all times.

I was talking with Ken, a friend of mine who had gone to one of the classes I had given on presence. Maybe about a month after the class we got together, and I asked him how the practice of presence was going. He said, "I do it, but I don't do it as often as I should." So I asked him, "How do you feel when you actually practice presence throughout the day, when you're taking those three conscious breaths?" He said, "In my company we have a managers' meeting every Thursday. There are roughly ten managers in the meeting and they're very chaotic. Everyone is talking over each other, getting loud, getting upset, getting frustrated. And I just get frustrated because you can't accomplish anything with everyone in a chaotic state. So I intentionally breathe, and when I breathe, it's like I can see through the chaos and I actually feel calm and at peace. All the noise just doesn't affect me. And that's the best part of practicing presence for me."

So I said, "Ken, you're allowing resistance to sabotage your peace because you can access that peace *all the time*—not just at your managers' meeting—by bringing in stillness, by taking three conscious breaths in a row, throughout the day, to access God's spiritual energy."

God's peace is available to us at any moment, but we have to do the work of bringing in stillness to access it. Going back to the parable of the hidden treasure, the man in the parable has to work in the field before he finds the treasure. But once he finds the treasure, his problems become meaningless. He's found something far beyond what he thought was possible—this is a treasure of true and lasting love, joy, and contentment. The peace of the present moment gives us access to that same treasure.

When we do the work necessary to be still inside, we experience God's spiritual energy within us.

Acceptance, nonresistance, and *appreciation* are essential tools in experiencing God's peace within us. When we use these tools to do the work—accept what is in nonresistance—our problems no longer have power over us. It opens the space that allows God's peace to flow through us. If we don't appreciate the power and peace of the present moment through the practice of presence, we block access to it.

Peace Is a Choice

We all *want* peace, but usually we don't *choose* it. Why is that? In some cases, it might be because we don't recognize it. Before I made the practice of presence primary in my life, if someone asked me, "Are you happy?" I would have absolutely said yes. But later, through the practice of presence, I realized that happiness is shallow compared to peace. Happiness comes and goes, but peace, a spiritual gift, is a taste of the eternal within us.

But most often we don't choose peace because most of us don't realize that we do actually have a choice. If we build a foundation—if we practice presence and experience God's peace—we will have confidence that we always have access because we have experienced the peace of the present moment over and over again. We cannot think our way into conscious presence. Choosing peace is an action.

How do we choose peace? The first thing we have to do is stop that voice in our head, all the compulsive thinking, before we can actually realize we have that option. Then our perception of reality changes because the screen of our ego has been lifted. When we put an end to the noise, we stop resistance because we're living in reality now. As the writer Byron Katie says, "When we stop opposing reality, action becomes simple, fluid, kind, and fearless."[6]

When I first made the conscious decision to make the practice of presence primary in my life over fifteen years ago, I would always start my day—as I still do—with the practice of presence for twenty minutes. But after that, throughout the day, I used to get frustrated and say to myself, "Why can't I just feel that calm and at peace all the time?" I realized that with all the distractions in my life, all the situations that come up in my business that may irritate or frustrate me, also the family dynamics that require patient thought and action, and all the daily distractions that pop up unexpectedly—the peace of the present moment is not a permanent state, and the only way to maintain a connection with God's spiritual energy within me is for me to choose to renew myself over and over again throughout the day by simply taking three conscious breaths. That basic practice of presence is the best decision I ever made.

We can't think our way into the peace of the present moment, but we can and do think our way into anxiety, stress, and worry through compulsive, negative thinking far too often. And when we allow that to happen, inner unease or even chaos lingers within us. It is important to remember that when we make the choice to practice presence, it is calm and peace that lingers within us. Then getting back to the peace of the present moment is easy. It literally takes only twenty seconds, three times, several times throughout the day. It is so simple and yet so powerful because it is being done to us when we bring in stillness and practice presence with the right intention—to connect with God's spiritual energy.

Peace Is the Kingdom

Jesus told us that "the kingdom of heaven is like what happens when a farmer plants a mustard seed in a field. Although it is the smallest of all seeds, it grows larger than any garden plant and becomes a tree. Birds even come and nest on its branches" (Matthew 13:31–32 CEV).

The kingdom of heaven is God's peace. It is not otherworldly, but rather within us and all around us all the time—and if we haven't experienced it, it can be easy to miss. As depth psychologist and former Catholic monk Thomas Moore explains, "[The] kingdom . . . is not overt, not even visible, and it is tiny. Yet it can change a life and alter the course of the world."[7] The Episcopal priest John Sanford says the kingdom "cannot be thought but can only be embraced, perhaps for a moment, in a mystical experience, for it far transcends personal consciousness and the limitations of the ego's thinking."[8]

The practice of presence is much like that mustard seed. It is so simple, so unobtrusive, so easy to fit into our lives. Yet as we practice regularly—as we continually experience the power of God's spiritual energy in our everyday lives—the practice of presence becomes so much more than a spiritual practice. We may become impatient in the beginning or resistant at times. But compare that to unconsciousness, where we create inner fears and conflicts that result in feeling lost and empty inside—which is more difficult to deal with. Eventually, through the power and peace of the present moment, the resistance and impatience stop, and we experience the unmistakable gateway to the kingdom of heaven, God's peace. It becomes essential to our well-being. The practice is simple, but its impact is profound.

MAKING MEANING OF THE MESSAGE

I believe at our core we all long for God's peace. But at the same time, we tend to be unaware of what is blocking true spiritual peace in our lives. No matter what our individual circumstances are, it is always unconsciousness when we flood our minds with compulsive, repetitive, negative thoughts, emotions, and reactions, and that causes us to lose access to the power and peace of the present moment. The peace of the present moment keeps us coming back and renews us throughout the day. We won't settle for getting lost in compulsive negative thinking. We know we have a choice. We stop mistaking that unconscious voice in our head for *who we are*. Our ego no longer has power over us. That is the greatest gift God has given us—his presence now, his peace. Presence is not a mind-set, but a surrender to the spiritual power of the present moment, which humbles us because we know we cannot do anything meaningful in our life without connecting to God's spiritual energy through stillness. That is when God changes us from the inside, which ultimately changes everything we do outside.

SET THE INTENTION

Father, the peace that you gave your son and in turn he gave to us is the only power that can stop our inner fears and conflicts.

PRACTICE PRESENCE

Bring in stillness and ask yourself the three questions to gauge your progress:

- Am I present now?

- How do I feel inside?

- Do I have a sense of peace within at some level?

See pages 10–11 for the details of this exercise or use the *Practicing Presence* app.

Answering Your Questions about Practicing Presence

What follows is a list of questions that have been asked by a diverse group of people—average working people, religious people, businesspeople, inmates in jail, homeless people, very well-educated people, and people who are not well educated. I've also included questions I have had myself. For each question I provide a direct answer to help you overcome a common obstacle or challenge to practicing presence. Hopefully this section will answer some questions you may have about this profound experience.

How does the practice of the practice of presence deepen our existing prayer practice?

If we want to be honest with ourselves, we have to ask: Why isn't prayer working as it should? Why isn't practicing our faith, such as going to church, working as it should? If it were working as it should—meaning that God's Spirit is guiding us—and his Spirit truly were guiding us, the inner fears, conflicts, and lack of self-esteem we experience would not be as rampant throughout our society. There wouldn't be so many people feeling hopeless, alone, and isolated. It just would not be the case. *It's not that prayer or practicing our faith has lost its power.* It is because most of us are not praying or practicing our faith as we should. When we pray, we have to ask ourselves: "Am I here now?" An example would be, when we say the Our Father. After we finish, we should ask ourselves: "How many thoughts went through my head when I was saying the Our Father?" I think we'd be surprised to find that quite a few thoughts went through our head. So we have to listen to what James says: A person in two minds is like the waves in the ocean being blown back and forth by the wind. The person is unstable. And James said, if we pray to God in two minds, don't expect anything from God (James 1:6–8). The practice of presence is our foundation that stops the noise and keeps us connected to our vibrant inner life. And the more we practice presence, the more aware we become of how we feel inside. The more aware we become, the easier we can sense negativity arising within us. And we are able to stop it before it takes over. That is the power of the practice of presence. Presence doesn't take the place of anything; it enhances everything. When we are present to God's Spirit within us, it restores the power of prayer and the power of practicing our faith—because we are not far from his constant presence within us and all around us. He is teaching us through the undeniable peace flowing through us when we are still inside.

What happens if I can't get still in three or five or seven breaths . . . or even one hour of breathing?

If that is the case, the first thing we have to look at is if we're breathing properly. Are we taking in the air, filling our lungs until we cannot fit any more air in? What happens when we don't do that is that we tend to breathe and think at the same time. When we do the breathing correctly and follow our breath and say the sacred word, it makes it much easier to focus on our breath, which leads us to stillness.

What if I lose confidence in the practice?

Usually we lose confidence in the practice if we haven't done it consistently. And if we haven't done it consistently, we haven't inner-conditioned ourselves. So the first thing our ego says is, "This doesn't work for me. There's no sense doing it. It just isn't working." That's the negative part. The positive part is this: When we actually go back and do it correctly and consistently, all of a sudden we get a breakthrough, where it's not only like it was before, but better. Then we have reached a different level of confidence in presence. And we have to go back and ask ourselves: "If I say it doesn't work, what am I going to go back to—creating more inner chaos?"

Are there particular challenges to practicing presence in public places, such as the grocery store or on the bus?

There aren't any challenges. And surprisingly, in those situations—on a bus, in a grocery store, in a car—it's almost easier to bring in stillness. In those situations, at times I've taken a couple of breaths but wind up breathing for fifteen minutes straight because I feel so different inside, so much calmness and peace.

Are there particular challenges to practicing presence in private?

The only challenge with practicing in private is to have the right intention and to do the practice properly. What we find is that if we are bored or distracted by something and then we practice presence correctly, suddenly we feel that sense of calm and peace within ourselves—that also is another breakthrough. What we thought was not going to happen actually happened, and we start to realize we didn't do it. It was done *to us* as we became still. That is the power of the present moment.

How do I explain the practice of presence to my family?

What I have done with my family and other families is this: If there is one thing we all can agree on, it is that when we are emotionally upset, when we may have resentments toward another person, when for no reason our mind just starts exploding with thoughts one after the other nonstop, when our self-esteem is diminished, it is always because of the inner negative dialogue inside of each of us, and none of us can say it doesn't happen to me. It happens to all of us. We also think we simply cannot stop all the inner chaos. The practice of presence does what we thought was impossible. When we are in emotional turmoil, practicing presence stops the inner fears and conflicts we create when we are outside the present moment, allowing our ego mind to guide us instead of our inner intelligence—which is God's Spirit within us in this moment and the only reality there is. It stops the chain of compulsive, repetitive, involuntary negative thinking, which is always followed by a chain of negative emotions and reactions.

How do I explain the practice of presence to my spiritual advisor?

What I would say to a spiritual advisor or a priest is that there are thousands of scripture readings that are powerful and full of wisdom. But for me there are three that sort out our relationship with God and how much he loves us. The first is Psalm 46:10: "Be still, and know that I am God." In the second, Jesus says in John, they all shall be taught by God (John 6:45). The third is when Jesus is asked what the greatest commandment is and he says, "Love the Lord your God with all your heart, soul, and mind. This is the first and most important commandment. The second most important commandment is like this one. And it is, Love others as much as you love yourself" (Matthew 22:37–40 CEV). And then he says I think the most important thing: All the law and prophets depend on these two commandments. How can we accomplish these things without stillness, without the experience of God's presence within us? First, how can we possibly become still? Second, how are we really going to believe that God is personally our teacher? And third, those two commandments are all love, love, love. But it's hard for us to love everybody. It's almost impossible unless there is a change in consciousness, unless we experience something that is beyond us. It isn't knowledge; it isn't an answer: It is an action. That's what presence is to me.

How do I ensure my intentions are on target for my practice?

We don't have to worry about a lot of intentions. There is one core intention—to connect with our vibrant inner life, God's Spirit within us, our inner intelligence. When we take care of the inside first, by connecting to Spirit, the outside takes care of itself. Any other intention is secondary to that. When we are truly consciously present, the outcome doesn't matter. Love has broken through. God is love.

If I am angry at God, can I still practice presence?

I've never actually had that experience, so it's hard to give an answer. But I do know this: We can't be angry and practice presence, because we've already put the screen of our ego between us and God. To practice presence as God wants us to, there has to be humility on our part. If someone came to me and said, "I'm angry at God, but I want to practice presence," I would tell them, "Do the practice correctly but your sacred word or words should be 'Father, please stop this anger. It is devouring me from the inside.' And I would just keep doing it until I can hear what he wants to teach me."

I'm so busy I forget to practice presence by taking three conscious breaths. How can I stop that?

When you realize that you forgot to practice presence, to consciously breathe, that's a good thing. When we realize that we've forgotten, we need to immediately take three conscious breaths, three times, or longer, until we feel that sense of our vibrant inner life, that calm within ourselves, as we slow down the inner negative dialogue. As we practice consistently, we are conditioning ourselves. And what keeps us coming back is that sense of inner calm and inner freedom. There is never a time during the day when we can't take at least three conscious breaths with the intention of connecting with our vibrant inner life. It doesn't interfere with anything, and it enhances every single thing.

Does this mean we have to breathe like this every day, forever, three times every hour or more? That's hard.

Actually it is not hard at all. It's our resistance that makes it *seem* hard. It's our ego trying to escape the present moment because it cannot guide us in the present moment. I've been practicing presence for over fifteen years, and breathing many times throughout the day is one of the greatest joys in my life because I don't just breathe when I am becoming emotionally upset about something. I breathe throughout the day when I feel good because it enhances my life and makes me feel even better. It increases the quality of everything I do. I feel connected. If we make the practice into a chore, then we miss the true power of presence. Every time we practice presence with the right intention, it's a renewal. It's a new beginning: the access to God's Spirit always that God has given us as a gift. It is a power we cannot connect to when we are in our unobserved mind, unconscious. What is really hard is dealing with the inner chaos we cause ourselves when our ego mind is just exploding with negative thoughts and emotions.

I'm a high-energy person. Will stillness be boring?

Actually, stillness is the opposite of boring. Practicing presence intensifies our energy. The energy has more depth because it is not ego-driven but Spirit-driven, which makes it much more personal. And just like for all high-energy people, myself included, there comes a time during the day when we simply get fatigued—physically or some inner conflict saps our energy. That does not happen in stillness. If a conflict comes, we know exactly how to face it, and we have the confidence to face it, because we know its origin. We made a problem personal, and we became the problem. As far as physical fatigue goes, we can be exhausted, but our inner vibrant life never loses its energy. We only connect with that power through stillness.

What do I do with my anger and resentments toward certain people?

The first thing we have to do is to bring in stillness to get a true perspective of reality. Resentments actually cause us inner pain. By bringing in stillness we stop that inner negativity and realize that God forgives us. And if God forgives us, we have to forgive ourselves and everyone else. Usually the people we resent aren't hurt by us. We ourselves are the ones who suffer from the resentments. If we have resentments or anger toward any person, we cannot be present at the same time because resentment and anger do not exist in the present moment; they are tied into the past. To accept the peace of the present moment, we have to let go of any resentments and any negative feelings toward every person. Unless we forgive as we have been forgiven, we will not be able to connect with our vibrant inner life. God's Spirit within us—that is what connects us to everyone.

When I feel emotionally upset and my mind is running, I think of the good things in my life, what's positive is my life, and that helps. Is that what you mean by presence?

No, that is not what I mean by presence. When we try to think positively about things in our life, it does give us some relief. But after a short time, all those negative emotions and reactions return. Presence is *the cure* because we're getting to the cause of all the self-created inner turmoil going on inside of us. By connecting with our vibrant inner life, God's Spirit within us, we realize we have an alternative, a contrast to our suffering, and we always have access to the peace that is in the present moment. When we experience God's peace, all those problems that we thought we had are just not that important compared to what we are experiencing.

What do you mean by the courage and the confidence to stop compulsively negative thinking?

As we begin to practice presence throughout the day, at times we're going to feel almost as though if we become present, we're going to miss something. But as we grow in the power of the present moment, we realize that the only thing we're going to miss is the misery we cause ourselves. We realize through our own experience, once our thoughts become compulsive and repetitive, they become useless and stress-producing. As we stop the inner negative dialogue through the practice of presence, we realize how powerful it is, and our confidence expands and expands.

"The practice teaches us"—what does that mean?

The practice of presence teaches us because it gives us a different perspective of reality. It shows us real life now, absent the inner chaos we sometimes create. By reacting to our life situation instead of living our life without the screen of our ego blocking our reality, we are free inside.

Why should I try it? Meditation just doesn't work for me, and the practice of presence is a form of meditation.

If we say that, aren't we just condemning ourselves to compulsive, repetitive, and involuntary negative thinking throughout the day? As Eckhart Tolle rightfully says, it's a terrible affliction not to be able to stop our mind from thinking. Usually we say that, not because we cannot meditate, but just because we have so much resistance to actually being still inside. That reminds me of something Richard Rohr said: Most people don't meditate because they don't want to be alone with someone they don't like. All of that changes with the consistent practice of presence. If we can be still for one minute, which we all have been, that means we can be still for one hour. And if we can be still for one hour, we can be still for one day. And just repeat that day for the rest of your life. God will take care of the rest.

What is the difference between meditation and the practice of presence?

Meditation means different things to different people. And there are many different forms of meditation. When we meditate, our intentions might be to have a better relationship with God, to calm ourselves down inside, to stop our mind from running, or stop our inner fears and also to feel better about ourselves. And there are many more reasons. It seems for most people, there may be many reasons why they're meditating, but just in talking to people who meditate, it seems that in too many cases they really don't know what they are looking for. Their intentions are good, but because they really don't know what they're seeking, many of them stop meditating because they're really not experiencing a recognizable change in their life. There is no inner calm or experience of presence at some level. The practice of presence is very specific. There is only one intention, there is only thing that matters, and that is to connect with our vibrant inner life, God's Spirit within us. That allows us to experience how we feel inside when we are still. And that is who we truly are. Without the distractions we cause in our unobserved mind, this is the experience that lets us know exactly what we are looking for: the calm that evolves into peace fills us with love. It's that experience at some level that lets us know that no matter what is happening in our life situation, it is secondary to what we are experiencing inside. We are not alone. And God told us exactly what we must do to experience his presence: "Be still, and know that I am God." When we become consciously present, what we are experiencing inside is unmistakable compared to how we feel when we are in our unobserved mind, where all of our inner negative dialogue begins. It is a shift in our awareness caused by the experience and reality of God's presence in our life. And we keep coming back to the practice of presence because we know there is no greater truth or power or gift as important as his presence. We know exactly what we're looking for and why. We do not create the inner change; it is being done to us when we are still.

When you say that through the practice of presence, "we know what we are looking for," how do we know what we are looking for?

The heart of the practice of presence is how unmistakably different we feel inside when we bring in stillness and experience the power and peace of the present moment. We experience a connectedness and a sense of peace at some level. We experience the difference in our inner well-being when we are consciously present compared to when we are unconscious, living through memory or anticipation, creating inner fears and inner conflicts within ourselves. We truly have a choice: to stay in our suffering or to stop our suffering. We will always choose the peace of the present moment.

I take three breaths, and right after my mind starts running— why?

The main reason for a quick return to a running mind is we're probably not doing the practice consistently enough to inner-condition ourselves. We're waiting too long in between taking the three breaths. If that happens, just return to taking conscious breaths. It doesn't matter how many you take—you can't take too many breaths, and the practice doesn't interfere with anything. When we are consciously breathing correctly, we're not going to have any issue with compulsive and repetitive thinking. Consciously breathing keeps us focused and present, and we realize how useless and stress-producing the repetitive thinking is. As we practice presence more consistently, our confidence in it changes. We know how to get back to reality.

How can the practice of presence help me cope with my fear of death?

All fear—whether it's fear of losing something, fear of being wrong, fear of being hurt, fear of being abandoned, or fear of being diminished—at the core is fear of death. Through the practice of presence, we realize our fears are in the future. That is why they cause us so much pain—they are not real now, and we cannot deal with a mind fiction. Through the practice of presence, we experience a taste of the eternal within ourselves that is God's Spirit within us, and that never dies. Once we experience the eternal within ourselves, the fear of death starts to diminish until it no longer has power over us.

Should we teach our children the practice of presence?

It is very important to teach the practice of presence to our children so that they can recognize the unconsciousness in our society, the harm it does to so many people, and the needless suffering it causes not only to other people, but also to ourselves. Teaching our children the practice of presence through our own example is a gift we can give them—knowing the cause of unconsciousness and how to connect with the power that stops it, God's spiritual energy within them. That power will enrich their lives continuously, but it's very important to remember that we cannot truly teach our children what we have not experienced ourselves.

Notes

Morning Practice of Presence Session

1. Kerstin Uvnäs-Moberg, Linda Handlin, and Maria Petersson, "Self-Soothing Behaviors with Particular Reference to Oxytocin Release Induced by Non-Noxious Sensory Stimulation," *Frontiers in Psychology* 5 (2014): 1529, doi:10.3389/fpsyg.2014.01529; Ellen Albertson, "Oxytocin: The Love Hormone," Dr. Ellen, February 9, 2018, https://drellenalbertson.com/oxytocin-the-love-hormone.

Chapter 1: The Unconscious Self

1. T. M. Luhrmann, "The Anxious Americans," *New York Times*, July 18, 2015, http://www.nytimes.com/2015/07/19/opinion/sunday/the-anxious-americans.html.

2. Kendra Cherry, "The Preconscious, Conscious, and Unconscious Minds," VeryWellMind, last modified June 15, 2019, https://www.verywellmind.com/the-conscious-and-unconscious-mind-2795946.

3. Thomas Merton, *Love and Living* (New York: Farrar, Straus and Giroux, 1979), 43.

4. Eckhart Tolle, "Free Yourself from Your Ego Armor," Oprah's Life Class, October 10, 2011, http://www.oprah.com/oprahs-lifeclass/eckhart-tolle-on-how-to-free-yourself-from-your-ego-armor.

5. Tolle, "Free Yourself from Your Ego Armor."

6. Thomas Merton, *The Waters of Siloe* (New York: Harcourt & Brace, 1949), 349.

7. Adapted from Richard Rohr, *Dancing Standing Still: Healing the World from a Place of Prayer* (Mahwah, NJ: Paulist Press, 2014), 70.

Chapter 2: Meeting God in the Moment

1. Henri J. Nouwen, *Bread for the Journey: A Daybook of Wisdom and Faith* (San Francisco: HarperOne, 2006).

2. Thomas Merton, *Disputed Questions* (New York: Harvest Books, 1985).

3. Christine Valters Paintner, *Lectio Divina—The Sacred Art: Transforming Words and Images into Heart-Centered Prayer* (Woodstock, VT: SkyLight Paths Publishing, 2011), 104.

4. Thomas Merton, *New Seeds of Contemplation* (New York: New Direction: 2007), 190.

5. Helen Mallicoat, "I Am," quoted in Tim Hansel, *Holy Sweat* (Nashville: W Publishing Group, 1987), 136.

Chapter 3: Stillness

1. Neringa Antanaityte, "Mind Matters: How to Effortlessly Have More Positive Thoughts," TLEX Institute, accessed June 28, 2019, https://tlexinstitute.com/how-to-effortlessly -have-more-positive-thoughts.

2. John Breck, "On Silence and Stillness," Orthodox Church of America, https://oca.org/reflections/fr.-john-breck/on-silence -and-stillness.

3. "Oprah Talks to Eckhart Tolle, *O, the Oprah Magazine*, May 2008, https://www.oprah.com/spirit/oprah-talks-to-eckhart-tolle/ all.

4. Eckhart Tolle, *Stillness Speaks* (Novato, CA: New World Library, 2003).

5. Peggy Ocalfon, *Escape from Anxiety: Supercharge Your Life with Powerful Strategies from A to Z* (Naples, FL: Stonewater Studio Books, 2015).

6. Richard Rohr said this at Soularize, the annual meeting of the Center for Action and Contemplation, in Grants, New Mexico, about ten to fifteen years ago.

7. Ronald Rolheiser, *Prayer: Our Deepest Longing* (Cincinnati, OH: Franciscan Media, 2013), chapt. 2.

8. Paula D'Arcy, *Sacred Threshold: Crossing the Inner Barrier to a Deeper Love* (New York: Crossroad, 2007).

9. Fr. Stan Bosch, ST, PsyD, LMFT.

10. Richard Rohr, "The Prayer of Quiet," *Huffington Post*, January 31, 2013; http://www.huffingtonpost.com/fr-richard-rohr /prayer-of-quiet-video_b_2591242.html?utm_hp_ref=religion.

11. Henri J. M. Nouwen, *Life of the Beloved: Spiritual Living in a Secular World* (New York: Crossroad, 2002).

Chapter 4: Accessing Presence

1. Richard J. Foster, *Life with God: Reading the Bible for Spiritual Transformation* (San Francisco: HarperOne, 2010).

2. Maggie Lyon, "The Top 10 Benefits of Spiritual Practice," *Huffington Post*, last modified March 28, 2012, http://www .huffingtonpost.com/maggie-lyon/spiritual-practice_b_1231569 .html.

3. Anthony de Mello, *The Heart of the Enlightened: A Book of Story Meditations* (New York: Image, 1997).

4. Commentary on the Gospel of John 121:4.

5. William Johnston, *Christian Zen: A Way of Meditation* (Bronx, NY: Fordham University Press, 1997),79, 115.

Chapter 5: Inner Conditioning

1. Debra Moffitt, "Tapping into Courage for Spiritual Change," Beliefnet, http://www.beliefnet.com/columnists /awakeintheworld/2012/01/tapping-into-courage-for-spiritual -change.html.

Chapter 6: Resistance

1. Eckhart Tolle, quoted in Tami Simon, "The Power of Now and the End of Suffering," Eckhart Tolle Now, https://www.eckharttollenow.com/article/The-Power-Of-Now-Spirituality-And-The-End-Of-Suffering.

2. Eckhart Tolle, quoted in Samuel Austin, "Life Consists Entirely of the Present Moment by Eckhart Tolle," Live Learn Evolve, October 21, 2014, https://livelearnevolve.com/the-present-moment-eckhart-tolle.

3. Vinita Hampton Wright, "Four Reasons We Resist Letting Go," Ignatian Spirituality, http://www.ignatianspirituality.com/24479/four-reasons-we-resist-letting-go.

4. Melissa Chu, "Stop Making Excuses and Start Being Honest with Yourself, Thrive Global, July 11, 2017, https://journal.thriveglobal.com/stop-making-excuses-and-start-being-honest-with-yourself-6312b473875b.

5. Connie Chapman, "Six Signs You're in the Process of Transformation (and How to Manage It)," ConnieChapman.com, July 9, 2014, https://conniechapman.com/6-signs-youre-in-a-process-of-transformation.

6. Rick Warren, "How to Remove and Replace Your Old Habits—Daily Hope with Rick Warren," Crosswalk.com, August 24, 2016, https://www.crosswalk.com/devotionals/daily-hope-with-rick-warren/daily-hope-with-rick-warren-august-24-2016.html.

7. Rebecca Barlow Jordan, "Six Reasons We Resist Change," Crosswalk.com, January 19, 2017, https://www.crosswalk.com/faith/spiritual-life/6-reasons-we-resist-change.html.

Chapter 7: The Courage to Stop Negative Thinking and Gossip

1. Steve Taylor, "Can You Stop Thinking?," *Psychology Today*, March 30, 2015, https://www.psychologytoday.com/blog/out-the-darkness/201503/can-you-stop-thinking.

2. Eckhart Tolle, *A New Earth: Awakening to Your Life's Purpose* (New York: Penguin, 2008).

3. Jack Levin and Arnold Arluke, *Gossip: The Inside Scoop* (New York: Plenum Press, 1987), 7.

4. David G. R. Keller, *Desert Banquet: A Year of Wisdom from the Desert Mothers and Fathers* (Collegeville, MN: Liturgical Press, 2011), 197.

5. Eckhart Tolle, "Dis-Identifying from the Thinking Mind," Tolle Teachings, http://www.tolleteachings.com/thinking -mind.html.

6. Jim Burklo, "Mindful Christianity," *Huffington Post*, last modified December 29, 2014, http://www.huffingtonpost.com /jim-burklo/mindful-christianity_b_6071700.html.

7. Burklo, "Mindful Christianity," http://www.huffingtonpost .com/jim-burklo/mindful-christianity_b_6071700.html.

8. Adapted from Karl Rahner, "Christian Living Formerly and Today," in *Theological Investigations VII*, trans. David Bourke (New York: Herder and Herder, 1971), 15.

9. Richard Rohr, "Willfulness versus Willingness," Richard Rohr's Daily Meditation, http://myemail.constantcontact.com /Richard-Rohr-s-Meditation--Willfulness-Versus-Willingness .html?soid=1103098668616&aid=3Rg1bZSVjLk.

Chapter 8: We All Want Peace

1. Rudolf Otto, *The Idea of the Holy* (New York: Oxford University Press, 1958), 6.

2. Carl Jung, *Civilization in Transition, The Collected Works of Carl Jung*, vol. 10 (Princeton, NJ: Princeton University Press, 1970), 651. See also "Jung and Numinosum," Jungian Center for Spiritual Sciences, http://jungiancenter.org/wp /jung-and-the-numinosum.

3. Carl Jung, *Psychology and Religion: West and East, The Collected Works of Carl Jung*, vol. 11 (Princeton, NJ: Princeton University Press, 1969), 274. See also "Jung and Numinosum," Jungian Center for Spiritual Sciences, http://jungiancenter.org /wp/jung-and-the-numinosum.

4. Carl McColman, "Two Types of Spiritual Peace," Patheos, August 6, 2012, http://www.patheos.com/progressive-christian /two-types-carl-mccolman-08-07-2012.

5. Eckhart Tolle, *The Power of Now: A Guide to Spiritual Enlightenment* (Vancouver: Namaste Publishing, 2004), 24.

6. Byron Katie with Stephen Mitchell, *Loving What Is: Four Questions That Can Change Your Life* (New York: Crown, 2002), ch. 1.

7. Thomas Moore, *Gospel—The Book of Matthew: A New Translation with Commentary—Jesus Spirituality for Everyone* (Woodstock, VT: SkyLight Paths, 2016).

8. John Sanford, *The Kingdom Within: The Inner Meaning of Jesus' Sayings* (San Francisco: HarperCollins, 1987), 173.

About *Practicing Presence—*
A Christian Way

The free app companion to *Choosing Presence: How to Access God's Peace and Release Fear, Anxiety, and Stress*

Practicing Presence—A Christian Way introduces modern Christians to a profound yet simple spiritual practice for sustaining a vibrant inner life that can be the salve to our modern plagues of stress, anxiety, worry, and fear. With an emphasis on cultivating a sustained daily commitment, this step-by-step guided breathing practice helps seekers of all levels of Christian involvement articulate a spiritual intention, bring in stillness, and connect with God's spiritual energy. The practice includes a brief reflective practice—three concise questions—to help you gauge your progress. The app includes a programmable hourly reminder feature.

Available for Android and iPhone

About the Author

Jim Heaney has been teaching the practice of presence from a Christian perspective for over twenty years, encouraging people of all ages to incorporate the practice into all areas of their lives—professional, relationships, sports, arts, health, and more—for greater spiritual and physical well-being.

Along with hosting home classes, he has presented at Ghost Ranch in Santa Fe, New Mexico; St. Benedict's Abbey in Still River, Massachusetts; the Center for Action and Contemplation's "Men as Learners and as Elders" annual gathering; Men's Rite of Passage events, where he is a teaching elder; the Illuman SoCal gathering of Orange County, a chapter of the international men's organization founded by Richard Rohr; and through the Catholic Detention Ministry, performing communion services to the inmates and teaching the practice of presence.

He is a member of St. Bonaventure Catholic Church in Huntington Beach, California, and is involved with such charitable organizations as the Friends of Dorothy Day, Isaiah House, and Collete's Children's Home.

Jim is the founder of Electronic Waveform Lab, manufacturer of the H-Wave device, the premier modality in the drug-free treatment of chronic pain. H-Wave has been featured in *Sports Illustrated*, *Los Angeles Times*, *USA Today*, ABC News, NBC Sports, and many other media, and has been used by many high-profile athletes in the NBA, NFL, NHL, PGA, professional tennis, and throughout college sports.

Jim lives with his wife, Patricia, in Huntington Beach, California.

www.ingramcontent.com/pod-product-compliance
Lightning Source LLC
Chambersburg PA
CBHW030012110426
42741CB00032B/407